L.B.S.C.R.

BRIGHTON
ATLANTICS

L.B.S.C.R.
BRIGHTON
ATLANTICS

JAMES S. BALDWIN

PEN & SWORD
TRANSPORT

Dedication:

This book is dedicated to my daughter Steff, who, as a
resident of Brighton, inspired me to write it.

First published in Great Britain in 2017 by
Pen & Sword Transport
An imprint of Pen & Sword Books Ltd
47 Church Street
Barnsley
South Yorkshire
S70 2AS

ISBN 978 1 78346 368 8

Typeset in Palatino by Pen & Sword Books Ltd.
Printed and bound in China by Imago.

Pen & Sword Books Ltd incorporates the imprints of Pen & Sword
Archaeology, Atlas, Aviation, Battleground, Discovery, Family
History, History, Maritime, Military, Naval, Politics, Railways, Select,
Social History, Transport, True Crime, and Claymore Press, Frontline
Books, Leo Cooper, Praetorian Press, Remember When, Seaforth
Publishing and Wharncliffe.

For a complete list of Pen and Sword titles please contact
Pen and Sword Books Limited
47 Church Street, Barnsley, South Yorkshire, S70 2AS, England
E-mail: enquiries@pen-and-sword.co.uk
Website: www.pen-and-sword.co.uk

Previous Publications:

Novels (Religious historical fiction)
The Child Madonna, Melrose Books, 2009
The Missing Madonna, PublishNation, 2012
The Madonna and her Sons, PublishNation, 2015

Novels (Railway fiction)
Lives on the Line, Max Books, 2013

Non-fiction (Railways)
The Toss of a Coin, PublishNation, 2014
A Privileged Journey, Pen & Sword, 2015
An Indian Summer of Steam, Pen & Sword, 2015
Great Western Eight-Coupled Heavy Freight Locomotives,
     Pen & Sword, 2015
Great Western Moguls and Prairies, Pen and Sword, 2016
The Urie and Maunsell 2-cylinder 4-6-0s, Pen and Sword, 2016
*Great Western Small Wheeled Outside Frame 4-4-0
     Tender Locomotives*, Pen and Sword, 2017

By the same author:
The Great Northern Atlantics, Pen & Sword, 2015 By James S. Baldwin

Non-fiction (Street Children)
The Other Railway Children, PublishNation, 2012
Nobody Ever Listened To Me, PublishNation, 2012

Cover photo: The H2 class Atlantics were built at Brighton Works
between 1911 - 1912 for main line service between London and the
Sussex Coast. Former LBSCR H2 class Atlantic Nº 2421 *South Foreland* is
seen at Newhaven shed in 1947. (Colour Rail Collection)

Back cover: H2 class Atlantic Nº 32426 *St Albans Head* is seen at Lewes,
waiting to depart via the then closed Bluebell Railway line to New Cross Gate
with 'The Wealden Limited' excursion on 14 August 1955. The special had
worked its way from Victoria to Lewis by a variety of locomotives, where *St
Albans Head* took over the train. (Colour Rail Collection /E. V. Fry)

ACKNOWLEDGEMENTS

I wish to thank the many people who have answered my questions, provided images and items of memorabilia for me to examine and who have recalled personal stories of some truly magnificent machines. In particular I should like to thank Fred Bailey, Roger Brassier, Jonathan Clay, M. Collins, Antony M. Ford, Ralph Gillam, R. H. N. Hardy, Mike Hudson, W. M. J. Jackson, David Jones, Norman Lee, Ernie Pay, Nick Pigott, John Scott-Morgan, Ted Talbot and Peter N. Townend. Last, but by no means least, my thanks go to my wife, Harriett, for her unfailing encouragement.

James S. Baldwin
London

Jonathan Clay 2008

Originally built by the LBSCR in 1911, N° 424, was named *Beachy Head* in 1926. This locomotive proved to be the last operational Atlantic locomotive to remain in traffic in this country and was finally withdrawn from service in 1958. It is now the subject of a reconstruction project on the Bluebell Railway. (Jonathan Clay)

CONTENTS

A fine view of the former London, Brighton & South Coast Railway's H2 class 4-4-2 Atlantic locomotive N° 32424, *Beachy Head*. It is this locomotive that is the subject of a recreation project at the Bluebell Railway in Sussex. (Author)

FOREWORD

nterest in the London, Brighton & South Coast Railway's Atlantic locomotives is increasing steadily with many articles and reports having appeared recently in the railway press. On the face of it this would seem to be out of all proportion to the number of these locomotives produced. Could it be due to the publicity surrounding the reconstruction of Nº 32424 *Beachy Head*, the last of this type of locomotive in service on British Railways withdrawn in April 1958? If so, this new book will be most warmly welcomed by those who wish to discover more about the locomotives and their designer Douglas Earl Marsh and his connection with its Great Northern Railway predecessors of which a static example, Nº 251, survives at the National Railway Museum.

I trust that my contribution to the Brighton Atlantic story will encourage readers to seek out the new *Beachy Head* on the Bluebell Railway and, once completed, savour the sights and sounds of this class of 4-4-2 that most had accepted would never be experienced again. We have to thank those who had the foresight to purchase the boiler that was the catalyst of this scheme, and the skilled engineers at Sheffield Park who have constructed the new locomotive by overcoming the many difficulties that have been encountered, not least the decline of British manufacturing industry preventing certain important traditional methods from being used. This in itself has introduced alternative manufacturing technology and skills to the heritage-railway movement and shows the way forward for other groups contemplating building new locomotives, of which there are several in the pipeline up and down the country.

David G. Jones, C.Eng, M.I.Mech.E.

INTRODUCTION

In the mid-nineteenth century the London, Brighton & South Coast Railway (LBSCR) was the principal railway linking London with the Sussex coast. It was formed in 1846, when the London & Croydon Railway merged with the London & Brighton Railway. The trains at that time were hauled by steam locomotives and took an hour and 45 minutes to travel from London Bridge (the original terminus in the capital) to Brighton. Initially almost all of the locomotives were named (indeed some were not even given numbers), but things changed when John Chester Craven was appointed Locomotive Superintendent in 1847. When he began to organise things he started by dropping the names — although names would be reintroduced when William Stroudley succeeded Craven at his retirement in 1869.

In contrast to Craven, Stroudley named almost every locomotive under his control, although he did draw the line at 0-6-0 goods locomotives. In the main, the names chosen were of towns and villages served by the LBSCR, with some European towns that came within (it was thought) the railway's sphere of the influence. There was little change to this naming principle when R. J. Billinton took over.

The LBSCR — known colloquially as 'The Brighton' — earned its glamorous reputation in its early years, the elegance of its magnificent Pullman cars being matched by the turnout of its locomotives, immaculate in their yellow livery, with shiny brass and copper adornments. However, when Marsh took over at Brighton in 1904 he changed the livery from bright gamboge (as seen on preserved locomotives such as *Gladstone* and *Boxhill*) to a much more subdued umber, and hereafter names were applied only to the railway's largest and most prestigious locomotives.

Largely on account of its extensive suburban network, the LBSCR was notable among railway companies in that its services were worked mainly by tank engines of the 4-4-2, 4-6-2 and 4-6-4 wheel arrangements. The Brighton liked its tanks, and when its handsome 4-6-4Ts were found to be unsteady at high speed they were modified to have well tanks built between the frames. This stopped their unsteadiness, although to preserve their fine appearance the side-tank sheeting was retained. While the 4-6-4Ts were the largest tank engines that worked on the

LONDON AND CROYDON RAILWAY, FROM NEW CROSS, DEPTFORD.

A view of the London & Croydon Railway (L&CR), as seen from New Cross, soon after the line had been opened in 1839. In July 1846 it merged with other railways to form the London Brighton and South Coast Railway (LB&SCR). Towards the top of the picture can be seen the brick viaduct of the London & Greenwich Railway (L&GR). (Author)

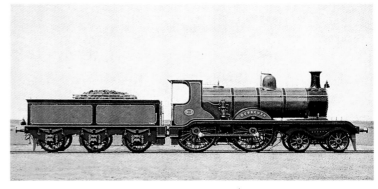

Brighton, the smallest were the famous Stroudley-designed 0-6-0 'Terriers', which, although a joy to behold, proved inadequate when required to haul heavy suburban trains, resulting in a lack of punctuality.

Although introduced by D. E. Marsh the LBSCR's 4-4-2 tender engines were actually of Great Northern Railway (GNR) design. Earlier in his career Marsh had been H. A. Ivatt's Chief Assistant at the GNR's Doncaster Works, where he was at the sharp end of railway development in a major railway organisation. When he later moved to Brighton Works, he became the Locomotive Superintendent of the LBSCR from 1905 to 1912. He needed a powerful express locomotive to cope with the ever-growing traffic on his railway and chose to use a proven design: the GNR's large-boiler Atlantic. With some slight modifications the Marsh Atlantics were a success.

Although the LBSCR formed the smallest of the three sections of the new Southern Railway, formed in 1923, it dominated the provision of railway services through much of the south of England feeding into London. Its termini at Victoria and London Bridge were linked to the

The Brighton line accrued much glamour in its early years of existence. Some of this stardom stemmed in the early years from the beauty and elegance of the locomotives in their immaculate yellow livery, shiny brass and copper adornments. Most, if not all, were individually named and here we see a B3 class 4-4-0 locomotive N° 213, *Bessemer*, as originally built. (Author)

A magnificent view of part of the large double-spanned, curved, glass and iron roof, covering the platforms of Brighton's Terminus Station. Spanning the tracks and rising 75 feet above the platforms is the glorious cast iron and glass train shed, which was erected from 1882 - 1883. Following the curvature of the tracks, the roof is supported on cast iron columns, some of which bear the name of the Midlands engineering firm, the Patent Shaft and Axletree Company of Wednesbury, which was located in the 'Black Country'. The company, which had won the contract to supply the ironwork, had all of the metalwork delivered by rail. It was erected above the existing train shed without a single day of train service operation being lost. The station was substantially renovated between 1999 and 2000. (Author)

Tank engines of the 4-4-2T, 4-6-2T and 4-6-4T wheel arrangements mainly worked the LBSCR's Brighton Line, along with its extensive suburban system. Indeed, such was the aesthetic 'mind-set' of the Brighton that when the handsomely designed 4-6-4T locomotives were found to be unsteady at high-speed, they were rebuilt with well-tanks between the frames. In order not to detract from their fine appearance, the side tank sheeting was maintained if not actually used. Here is a contemporary image of a 4-6-4T locomotive N° 333, *Remembrance*, leaving Victoria Station, London, with the '*Southern Belle*' Pullman service to Brighton. (Author)

As Douglas Earle Marsh had been involved in creating the GNR's large boiler Atlantic engines, he approached Doncaster, who provided Brighton Works with a full set of Atlantic tender locomotive drawings although the 'Brighton Line' version was slightly different from the GNR's large boiler design. The Brighton engines became known as H1 class. Here is the GNR's N° 251, which was the first large boiler Atlantic 4-4-2 engine to run in this country. It was this design that the Brighton Atlantics were based upon. (Author)

coast at Brighton, and an intricate network of lines sprang up to serve Surrey, Sussex, west Kent and east Hampshire, making it one of the most important providers of commuter services into the capital.

The main line from London Bridge to Brighton, just over 50 miles in length, was sometimes described as an 'outer-suburban railway' on account of its considerable commuter traffic. But, with its 'South Coast' line extending from Portsmouth to Hastings, together with its network of lines in Sussex, the LBSCR was so very much more than that. It was normal for railway employees to show

loyalty to their parent companies and the men showed pride and real affection for their employer. Even with uncomfortable and late running trains, the passengers also had affection for their small and compact railway. This affection seemed to continue long after the Grouping of 1923.

Like most other railways of the early twentieth century, the LBSCR needed a new design of fast and powerful express locomotive. Having been actively involved in creating the GNR's successful large-boiler Atlantic, Marsh approached Doncaster Works, which willingly provided Brighton Works with a full set of Atlantic drawings. These were amended only slightly in 'red ink' for use on the Brighton line, and the resultant locomotives thus closely resembled

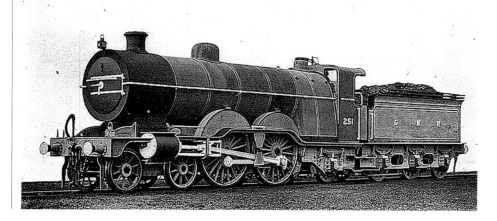

The National Railway Museum's 0-4-2 engine *Gladstone*, is finished in the livery known as Stroudley's improved engine green, which was actually an ochre colour, not green. This is historically attributed to colour-blindness, an affliction from which William Stroudley reportedly suffered. The actual shade of the livery has been much disputed, with opinions ranging from a more yellow type of livery, to a livery closer to brown. The first member of the class, N° 214 *Gladstone*, was preserved as a static exhibit thanks to the efforts of the Stephenson Locomotive Society and is normally on display in the NRM, York. *Gladstone* is the only former LBSCR tender locomotive to be preserved, as all the other preserved locomotives - ten A1 class/A1x class 'Terriers', one E1 class and an E4 class are tank engines. (Author)

PLATE XLIV.

WIDENING OF THE VICTORIA BRIDGE, PIMLICO..

SIR CHARLES FOX, ENGINEER.

FIG. 5.

FIG. 6

FIG 7.

FIG. 8

FIG. 5.

132. 3½

FIG. 4. SECTION.A.B.

82'.0"

Grosvenor Bridge, originally known as Victoria Railway Bridge, was first constructed in 1860 by the Victoria Station & Pimlico Railway, at a cost of £84,000, to carry trains into Victoria Station. The Victoria Station & Pimlico Railway was an early British railway company incorporated by an act of parliament in July 1858 to build a railway line connecting the existing London, Brighton & South Coast Railway terminus in Battersea to a new terminal at Victoria Station; hence this bridge over the River Thames. It was the first railway bridge across the Thames in central London and the engineer, Sir John Fowler, was the chief engineer for the Forth Railway Bridge, which opened in 1890. Here are details of the iron-work as used when the bridge was widened. (Author)

the GNR locomotives. The Brighton differences were different boiler wash-out hole positions, a Brighton-style chimney was required and a larger cab was provided for the footplate crew. The locomotives were built by Kitson & Co of Leeds and formed the LBSCR's H1 class. Five locomotives were delivered, the first appearing in December 1905. They were numbered 37-41, all being initially unnamed, but in June 1913 Nº 39 was named *La France* and was used to haul the train conveying Raymond Poincaré, the French President, from London to Portsmouth. This name was retained until the locomotive was renamed *Hartland Point* by the Southern Railway in January 1926, the other Brighton Atlantics also being named at around this time.

The success of the H1s having been recognised, the LBSCR decided to build six more Atlantics, and these were classified H2. Built at Brighton, they were very similar to the H1s save that they were superheated; in LBSCR days the

H1s were saturated, being fitted with superheated boilers only after the Grouping. None of the H2s were named by the LBSCR, but in SR days all were named after South Coast landmarks. The two classes were easily distinguishable, the H1s having the footplate swept up over the cylinders and down

again, ahead of the driving-wheel splashers, whereas on the H2s the footplate remained level until just ahead of the firebox.

The H1 and H2 Atlantics were the largest tender engines built for the LBSCR and, indeed, continued to provide good service to its successors, the Southern Railway and British Railways. They displayed a trait of sometimes stopping at 'top dead centre', being unable to move forward or backward, but the same problem was encounter years later in O. V. S. Bulleid's sleeve-valve experiments with 'H1' Nº 2039 *Hartland Point*, so presumably it was a quirk of the 4-4-2 wheel arrangement rather than the valve gear.

Nº 32424 *Beachy Head* became the last 4-4-2 tender engine to operate anywhere in the UK in normal revenue-earning service. This ex-LBSCR H2 performed its final public duty on 13 April 1958, when it worked the outward leg of the RCTS 'Sussex Coast Limited'

An early picture of the superb terminal station at Queen's Road, Brighton. The site is half a mile from and seventy feet above the sea shore and involved considerable excavation work to create a reasonable gradient from Patcham Tunnel. The gentlemen in top-hats, horse drawn carriages on the platform, four-wheeled coaches and magnificent gas lamps all give a splendid insight into a bygone era. (Author)

This LBSCR 4-4-2 Atlantic Nº 39 was built by Kitson's of Leeds, in January 1906. Following its use on the train for a State visit of the French President, it was named *Le France* from June 1913 to January 1926. It was the only H1 or H2 class Atlantic to carry a name in LBSCR days. (Author)

The front cover of a timetable for 'Brighton Line' trains advertises the 'Southern Belle' Pullman service to Brighton. (Author)

On 5 October 1952, the London Branch of the RCTS ran a tour called 'The Brighton Works Centenary Special' from Victoria to Brighton and back again. The train was worked by Brighton Atlantic N° 32424, Beachy Head. The outward journey to Brighton was completed in 58 minutes 48 seconds and the return was achieved in 60 minutes 13 seconds for the 50.9 miles, with the train keeping very close to the tight schedule. There was a permanent way check in the East Croydon area in the down direction, which caused a loss of time between Windmill Bridge and Coulsdon North, but this was later made up. The up-train reached 80 mph near Horley but was checked in the London area, although it nevertheless arrived on time. Here we see N° 32424, Beachy Head waiting to leave Brighton for the return trip to London. (Antony M. Ford)

railtour, the train comprising seven coaches, among them a 12-wheel Pullman car, Myrtle. Starting from Victoria Station, Beachy Head worked the train to Newhaven Harbour, running via East Croydon, Haywards Heath and Lewes. After the tour Beachy Head moved to

Brighton locomotive shed for the very last time. It then travelled to Eastleigh Works, after which it was withdrawn, having been the last Atlantic express passenger locomotive to run in ordinary service in Great Britain. All is not lost, however, for upon completion

of a new Beachy Head locomotive at the Bluebell Railway it will be possible to relive some of the best of the memories of the Brighton.

Here are the frames of the new build Atlantic Beachy Head, sitting on the bogie and trailing wheel-sets, as seen at Sheffield Park on 13 June 2012. At this time the group were still awaiting the driving wheels from Ian Riley. This view also shows one cylinder cover and one valve chest cover fitted to the cylinders, as well as the anti-vacuum valves just under the smokebox saddle. (Fred Bailey)

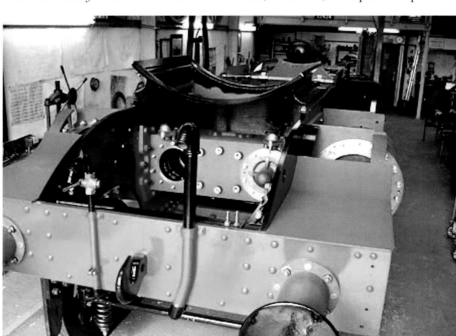

Chapter 1

ORIGINS OF THE ATLANTIC LOCOMOTIVE

I f you call a steam locomotive an Atlantic, you are using part of a commonly approved system of railway shorthand used to describe the wheel arrangement of a steam locomotive. In use from 1900, it was devised by an American, Frederick Methvan Whyte, who was born on 2 March 1865 and lived until 1941. He worked for the New York Central Railroad as a mechanical engineer. The use of 'Whyte notation' was encouraged by an editorial published in the *American Engineer* magazine and the *Railroad Journal* of

December 1900. Frederick Whyte's system first counts the number of leading wheels of a locomotive, followed by the number of driving wheels and finally the number of trailing wheels, with the groups of numbers being separated by dashes. So that, using Whyte notation, if a steam locomotive for example has two sets of leading axles — that is the four leading wheels in front, followed by two sets of coupled driving axles — that is the four middle sets of wheels, followed finally by one trailing axle — which

consists two wheels, this locomotive will be described as a 4-4-2.

The first use of the 4-4-2 wheel arrangement was for an experimental double-firebox locomotive built in 1888 to the design of George Strong at the Hinkley Locomotive Works in Boston, Massachusetts; however, the locomotive was not deemed to be successful and was scrapped soon afterwards. The 4-4-2 wheel arrangement was given the name of Atlantic after the second type of American-built 4-4-2 tender engines that were built. They

In the early 1890s, many American railroads adopted the 4-4-2 Atlantic type wheel arrangement, as these engines provided a fast and reliable service to such places as Atlantic City and New Jersey. Here is N° 350, a 4-4-2 Atlantic built for the Pennsylvania-Reading Seashore Lines. The photo shows well the 4-4-2 Atlantic wheel arrangement and the wide Wootten style firebox, which gave inspiration to the GNR Atlantics. (Author)

"Flying Scotchman" G.N.R.
NEAR HATFIELD

The first 4-4-2 locomotive to run in this country was built by the Great Northern Railway (GNR) and was numbered Nº 990. It was released to traffic in May 1898 and was a sensation in the world of railways. Classmate Nº 879, was released to traffic in June 1900 and it survived until 12 August 1936, when it was withdrawn from service and scrapped. (John Scott-Morgan)

were constructed by the Baldwin Locomotive Works in 1894, for use on the Atlantic City Line of the Philadelphia & Reading Rail Road. Known for its casinos, gambling, conventions and leisure, Atlantic City also served as the inspiration for the original version of the board game Monopoly. Then, on 20 July 1904, train Nº 25, a regularly scheduled service from Kaighn's Point in Camden, New Jersey, to Atlantic City, NJ, with Philadelphia & Reading Railway 'P-4c' 4-4-2 Nº

334 and five passenger carriages, set a new speed record, completing the 55.5-mile journey in 43 minutes, at an average speed of 77.4mph. The 29.3 miles between Winslow Junction and Meadows Tower — just outside Atlantic City, was covered in 20 minutes, at a speed of 87.9mph. During the short segment between Egg Harbor and Brigantine Junction the train was alleged to have reached 115mph. It was runs such as this that earned the 4-4-2s a notoriety, with the

result that locomotives of this wheel arrangement became known as Atlantics.

The Baldwin Locomotive Works' ideas on 4-4-2 tender engines, which were very successful, were soon copied in the UK, initially by H. A. Ivatt of the Great Northern Railway with his 'Klondike' design of 1898. These locomotives were quickly followed by the Lancashire & Yorkshire Railway's Class 7 locomotives built to the design of John Aspinall. The

The next development of British Atlantic design was the large boiler Atlantic, of which, N° 286, was an example. It is seen here hauling a train on the East Coast main line, c.1910. (John Scott-Morgan)

The GNR also had tank versions of the Atlantic 4-4-2 type of wheel arrangement. N° 1542 was released for traffic during July 1907, in GNR days. Here it is seen numbered as N° 4542 as was the case during its LNER days. This particular engine was so successful that it worked right through to British Railways days where it became N° 67392. It was withdrawn from service at New England depot in October 1956. (Author)

The second Atlantic to be constructed by D. E. Marsh was Nº 38, which was completed in December 1905 by Kitson's of Leeds. It was finally withdrawn from service in July 1951 and had by then been named *Selsey Bill* and had been renumbered to become Nº 32038. (Author)

next development of British-built Atlantics was the large-boiler Atlantic design built by the GNR, which also built tank engines with the same wheel arrangement. Later it was adopted by Douglas Earle Marsh after he had moved from the GNR to became Locomotive, Carriage & Wagon Superintendent on the London, Brighton & South Coast Railway, a total of 11 express passenger Atlantics being constructed for the high-speed luxury Pullman services on the Brighton line, where they were much admired and appreciated.

THE LONDON, BRIGHTON, & SOUTH COAST RAILWAY

EXPRESS PASSENGER LOCOMOTIVE, No. 38

DESIGNED BY MR. D. EARLE MARSH, M.INST.C.E.

BOILER	Length . . . . 16' 3⅞"	FIRE BOX	Length . . . . 5' 11"	DIAMETER OF WHEELS	Bogie . . . . 3' 6"	WEIGHT IN WORKING ORDER	Engine . 67 0
	Diameter . . . 5' 6"		Width . . . . 6' 9¼"		Coupled . . . 6' 7½"		Tender . 39 10
					Trailing . . . 3' 6"		Total . . Tons 106 10
CYLINDERS	Diameter . . . 1' 6½"	HEATING SURFACE	Tubes . . 2318 sq. ft.	GRATE AREA . . . . . 31 sq. ft.			
	Stroke . . . 2' 2"		Fire box . . 141 „	WORKING PRESSURE	200 lb. per sq. inch.	WATER CAPACITY . . . 3500 galls.
TUBES	No. 246		Total . 2459 sq. ft.			COAL CAPACITY . . . . 4 tons.

To classify a steam engine as an Atlantic, it has to have a 4-4-2 wheel arrangement - consisting of four leading wheels on two axles, usually in a leading bogie, four powered and coupled driving wheels on two axles and two trailing wheels on one axle, usually in a trailing truck. This configuration of wheels on a steam engine is commonly known as an Atlantic.

Here we see I1 class 4-4-2T Atlantic tank locomotive number 2 in LBSCR days at Battasea Yard. (John Scott-Morgan)

Chapter 2

CONSTRUCTION OF THE BRIGHTON LINE

Early in the nineteenth century, a new-fangled mode of transport on a public transport system which did not use animal traction power was starting to spring up all over the country, and those in the south of England were as eager as those in the north to be in at the start of the action as well. The origins for a railway between

Here is the coat of arms of the London, Brighton & South Coast Railway (LBSCR), which was formed by Act of Parliament on 27 July 1846, through the amalgamation of the London and Brighton Railway (L&BR), which had opened in 1841 and a number of other pre-existing railway companies, including the London & Croydon Railway (L&CR), which opened in 1839. (Author)

London and Brighton reaches right back to as early as 1823 (the year the Liverpool & Manchester Railway Co was founded), the first proposal being published for a 'communication' to be constructed between 'the Metropolis' (London) and the ports of Shoreham, Brighton, Rochester, Chatham and Portsmouth, but this plan was not developed.

With the passing in 1837 of the London & Brighton Railway Act authorisation was given to proceed with the construction of what would eventually become the principal route from London to the South Coast. Various other railway companies then sprang up in the area, *viz*:

> The London & Croydon Railway, formed in 1836 and opened in 1839

The Croydon & Epsom Railway, formed in July 1844 and still under construction (as an atmospheric railway) at the time of amalgamation

The Brighton & Chichester Railway, formed in 1844 and opened in stages between November 1845 and June 1846

The Brighton, Lewes & Hastings Railway, formed in February 1844 and opened in June 1846

Two of these companies — the Brighton & Chichester and the Brighton, Lewes & Hastings — were smaller independent railways purchased by the London & Brighton Railway (LBR) in 1845, while the Croydon & Epsom was largely owned by the London & Croydon (LCR). But the shareholders of the LBR and the LCR were dissatisfied with the early returns from their investments and brought about the amalgamation of all these odd railway companies in the region, much against the wishes of the boards of directors of the various companies. So, through the amalgamation of the LBR, which had opened in 1841 and a number of other existing railway companies,

the London, Brighton & South Coast Railway (LBSCR), was formed by Act of Parliament on 27 July 1846.

The LBSCR remained in existence for 76 years, until 31 December 1922, when it was wound up as a result of the Railways Act 1921, which was 'intended to stem the losses being made by many of the country's 120 railway companies, move the railways away from internal competition and to retain some of the benefits which the country had experienced from a Government controlled railway system, during and after the First World War'. The Brighton company's lines and assets were combined with those of the London & South Western Railway (LSWR) and the South Eastern & Chatham Railway (SECR) to form a new company, the Southern Railway (SR).

The Croydon Canal

Part of a scheme to link the London docks with Portsmouth, the Croydon Canal was authorised by Act of Parliament in 1801. The canal was originally intended to extend northwards to Rotherhithe, but the simultaneous construction of the Grand Surrey Canal provided a convenient access route. It was

The London & Brighton Railway (L&BR), built a passenger station, goods station, locomotive depot and railway works on a difficult site on the northern edge of Brighton. This site was a half-mile from and seventy feet above the sea shore and the construction involved considerable excavation work to create a reasonable gradient from Patcham Tunnel. This view shows the station forecourt showing David Mocatta's original building. The passenger station which incorporated the head office of the railway company, was a three-storey building in an Italianate style and was built between 1839-1840. This building, which still stands, has been largely obscured by later additions. The platform accommodation was built by John Urpeth Rastrick and consisted of four pitched roofs. The station opened for trains to Shoreham on 11 May 1840 and in September 1841, it started running services to London. (Author)

Located at Betts Park, Anerley is the last trace of the Croydon Canal. The Croydon Canal was built in the early nineteenth century, running from the Grand Surrey Canal, north of the present New Cross Gate station, to a basin located at the site of the present West Croydon Station. It was later bought by a railway company and much of its trackbed was used by what became the London, Brighton & South Coast Railway's main line south. Where the canal swung off the straighter course of the present railway, it was largely built over. The only other surviving piece of canal infrastructure is its reservoir which is located half a mile south-west and which is now called South Norwood Lake. (Author)

9.25 miles long and opened on 22 October 1809. It had 28 locks in the first 5 miles from Deptford and reached Croydon at a point now occupied by West Croydon Station. The Croydon Canal linked up with the Croydon, Merstham & Godstone Railway, which itself was connected to the Surrey Iron Railway, enabling the canal to be used to transport stone and lime from workings at Merstham right up to the centre of London. Although intended to reach Epsom the canal was never extended south-west.

The canal was originally planned to have two inclined planes — which consist of a flat supporting surface tilted at an angle, with one end higher than the other, used as an aid for raising or lowering canal barges or boats up the side of a hill. But the canal was eventually built with 28 locks, arranged in two flights instead. To keep the canal supplied with water, reservoirs were constructed at Sydenham and South Norwood — the latter still exists as South Norwood Lake in a public park. The canal was 34ft wide and had a maximum depth of 5ft. By 1811 some 22 barges were plying the canal. The barges were 60ft long and 9ft wide and could carry about 30 tons of goods, which consisted mainly of timber. After the initial flights of locks most of the canal followed the 161ft contour. The final two locks at Croydon Common raised the canal to the 174ft contour and because there was no natural source of water, a steam pumping station was built at the foot of the locks to pump water up to the summit pound. The canal, which was 9¼ miles long, was never a success and closed in 1836, mainly

due to insufficient water. It was the first canal to be abandoned by an Act of Parliament.

The useless canal was bought up on 21 July 1836 and was sold to the London & Croydon Railway Co for £40,250 1s, the one shilling being nominal compensation for the profits that the canal was in fact not making. A new railway line was constructed upon much of its former route for part of the railway line between London Bridge and West Croydon — the present-day station of which is located on the site of the original canal basin.

The new route branched away from the London & Greenwich Railway at Corbett's Lane Junction and ran along the former canal bed whenever possible, up the New Cross bank for over 2 miles, to the old canal summit at Forest Hill. During the following year the London & Croydon Railway obtained an Act of Parliament by which it had a station of its own constructed alongside that of the London & Greenwich Railway at London Bridge, although it did use the Greenwich's railway tracks for access until 1842.

A section of the original Croydon Canal (which is some 190yd long) has been completely rebuilt with a concrete base and sides and now forms an ornamental feature in Betts Park, Anerley Road, Anerley. The original canal route curved around the contours here at Anerley and so this section was considered to be unsuitable for further use by the railway company. Traces of the bridge over the canal route under Anerley Road can still be seen. Another survivor of the former canal is that of South Norwood

Lake, which is located quite close to Betts Park. It was built as a reservoir to supply the Croydon Canal but is now used for recreational purposes.

The London & Greenwich Railway

Greenwich was the home of royalty, for in 1447 a royal palace was built by Humphrey, Duke of Gloucester, on the banks of the River Thames, where it became the principal royal palace for 200 years. In 1491 it was the birthplace of Prince Henry (later King Henry VIII). He married Catherine of Aragon and the palace became the birthplace of Princess (later Queen) Mary in 1516. Afterwards, he married Anne Boleyn and their daughter, Princess (later Queen) Elizabeth, was born there in 1533. He also married Anne of Cleeves there in 1540. The palace fell into disrepair during the Civil War and was later used as a biscuit factory

The London and Greenwich Railway (L&GR), was opened in London between 1836 and 1838. It was the first steam railway to operate in the capital, the first steam railway to be built specifically for passengers and the first elevated railway system. The railway approached the capital along a viaduct which was 3.75 miles long and which consisted of 878 brick arches. (Author)

The London and Croydon Railway (L&CR), was an early railway in England. In 1839 and 1846, it merged with other railways to form the London, Brighton and South Coast Railway (LBSCR). This 1908 map shows the junction with the London and Greenwich Railway (L&GR) at Corbetts Lane, Bermondsey to New Cross Gate. (Author)

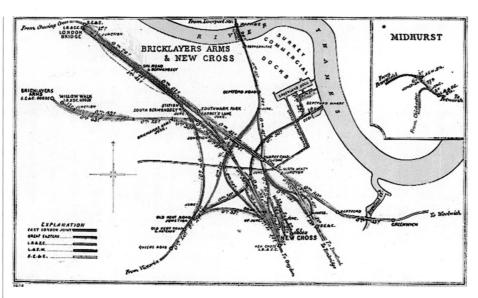

and a prisoner-of-war camp. Most of the palace was demolished until construction of the Royal Hospital for Seamen was built between 1696 and 1712. Designed by Sir Christopher Wren, the hospital closed in 1869. Between 1873 and 1998 it was the Royal Naval College. Greenwich is also famous for the Royal Observatory, which overlooks the Prime Meridian (0° longitude), and hence World Time is set to Greenwich Mean Time. But with all of this going on in 1836, Greenwich was still an independent market town in Kent and was of sufficient importance to be the destination of the first proper railway in London.

The London & Greenwich Railway, opened in stages between 1836 and 1838, was the first steam-hauled railway in the capital, the first to be built specifically for passengers rather than goods and the first elevated railway to be constructed anywhere in the world. When built it traversed a landscape of market gardens and nurseries, with little evidence of

industrialisation. The centre of the town was partly protected from industrial changes by the Royal Park and associated buildings.

The first part of the railway was opened in February 1836 and was the section located between Spa Road, Bermondsey, and Deptford. At the first Deptford Station the layout was set up so that horse-drawn carriages could drive up to platform level via the inclined plane, which still survives, running parallel to Deptford High Street on the south side of the present station, (opened in 1926).

The idea of a railway from London to Greenwich to be built on a viaduct, came from the engineer Colonel George Thomas Landmann and entrepreneur George Walter. The line was elevated to avoid the numerous level crossings, over the myriad streets which were already taking hold in the south of London. The intention had been for the line to descend to ground level, after crossing the Grand Surrey Canal, but this was opposed by parliament

and so it remained on course and elevated, at least as far as Deptford Creek, where it crossed the River Ravensbourne over a drawbridge.

On 25 November 1831 a company was floated which obtained the necessary Parliamentary approval in 1833. Work started on the foundations in February 1834 and the first experimental trains ran in 1835. The structure was not, however, completed until December 1836, due to the delays in obtaining materials for the Bermondsey Street bridge, near London Bridge.

During 1836 some 60 million bricks were required to complete the construction of the viaduct at London Bridge station, 400 navvies using more than 100,000 bricks per day. These were all made at Sittingbourne, Kent, and were transported to the huge building site by Thames barge.

The whole finished structure is carried on a 878-arch viaduct, the world's longest brick-built structure. As constructed the viaduct included a 'tree-lined pedestrian boulevard' where pedestrians could walk for a 'penny toll'. Subsequently however, to increase the number of tracks, the viaduct was widened over this boulevard, except for a stretch between Deptford and Greenwich, where sections of the footpath including Mechanics' Passage, since renamed as Resolution Way, are the only substantial surviving sections of 'boulevard' walkway, which flanked the original railway viaduct in 1836. It extends to Deptford Church Street, with small businesses in many of the arches and continues through the Crossfield Estate.

The terminus of the LGR at Greenwich was moved to its present

This atmospheric shot looking towards the entrance to London Bridge Station has so many things in it that are all but history now. The image was taken after the viaduct had been widened, but was before electrification had taken hold. Looking from the left we see: A non-corridor compartment engine hauled train; non-electrified lines; many Stroudley designed tank engines scurrying about; a gantry mounted signal box; semaphore signals, un-braked goods wagons full of coal and a turntable - its all gone now! (Author)

location in 1877, in preparation for the extension of the line to Dartford via Maze Hill. Greenwich station stands virtually as completed in 1878. The building is a neat two-storey brick building of seven bays with Portland stone ornamentation, fronted by a large courtyard. The full-length canopy has long since gone, but the corbels are still visible. More recently, the arrival of the Docklands Light Railway at Greenwich station has increased the usage of this landmark station considerably.

As the viaduct was constructed, stations were also included in this vast construction project and included the stations of London Bridge, Spa Road, closed in 1915, Bermondsey and Deptford. A further station on top of the viaduct at Southwark Park was opened in 1902, but this was closed during 1915.

The London & Croydon Railway

Following the successful opening of the Stockton & Darlington Railway and the Liverpool & Manchester Railway in 1825 and 1830 respectively several schemes were put forward for railways to be constructed in the South East of England. The London & Croydon Railway proposed a plan to build an 8.75-mile route between a junction with the LGR at Corbett's Lane, Bermondsey, the LCR trains using the LGR tracks for 2 miles from the terminus at London Bridge to the thriving market town of Croydon in Surrey. The first 3 miles of route from Croydon to Anerley followed the alignment of the unsuccessful Croydon Canal, West Croydon station and locomotive depot being built on the site of the former canal basin.

The line was authorised by Act of Parliament in July 1835, and the company purchased the redundant Croydon Canal bed for the route of its track. Before it had finished building its line the company had entered into agreements with two other railways: the South Eastern Railway, which had agreed to extend its line from Croydon to Dover, and the London & Brighton Railway, which joined the LCR at Norwood Junction. Although the LCR opened in 1839 it was merged along with other railways in the region to form the LBSCR in July 1846.

During 1838 and 1839 the LCR constructed a junction which connected the LGR's line, with the viaduct leading to its own 800ft viaduct at a point located shortly after Corbett's Lane, Deptford. Thereafter the LCR shared the LGR's route to London Bridge. As a

The Croydon Canal, ran from New Cross to the site of West Croydon Station. As it passed through South Norwood, pubs sprang up near its course. The Jolly Sailor Station which opened in 1839, was built by the London and Croydon Railway and was also a pub. It was listed as 'Jolly-Sailor near Beulah Spa' on fare lists and timetables. The station, which was renamed '*Norwood*' in 1846, was immediately adjacent to a level crossing over Portland Road, making it slightly further north than the site currently occupied by Norwood Junction. (Author)

direct result of this reorganisation, 'Corbett's Lane Junction' became one of the first major railway junctions in the world. For its operation, a 'policeman' was stationed at the junction to control the movements of the trains passing through. Not too long afterwards, the policeman was situated at the top of a wooden tower which was situated on the viaduct, to give him better visibility. The 'Corbett's Lane Lighthouse', as it was known, was the precursor of the modern-day signal box.

The LCR's line into London, already shared with the LGR, was from 1841 also shared with the London & Brighton Railway and from 1842 and was due to be further shared with the South Eastern Railway. It thus became obvious that the original viaduct into London Bridge would be inadequate to share the ever-increasing traffic of four railway companies. The solution was for the LGR to construct a second viaduct adjoining the south side of the original viaduct as far as Corbett's Lane Junction and provide two further tracks. The tracks on this southern viaduct were later leased by the LBSCR as successor to both the LCR and the LBR.

The SER leased the LGR from 1845 and gave the company control of its main line into London and obtained powers to widen the viaduct even further, with the addition of yet a further two lines for 2.65 miles but this time on the north side of the original viaduct, to accommodate the SER's main line. This work was completed by 1850.

The LGR's directors originally envisaged using the viaduct arches

for low cost housing, but they were soon dissuaded of the plan. The arches are today extensively used for light-engineering workshops, scrap dealers and as various lockups. In recent years some of the arches have even been used for fashionable restaurants and nightclubs.

Beginnings of the Brighton line

There were engineer's lines and there were contractor's lines, and the Brighton was an engineer's line. The Brighton Railway was originally projected by Sir John Rennie, and it took him nine years to get the scheme adopted. With his assistants, Grantham and Jago, he surveyed the route and originally placed his terminus at Kennington Park, running his route through Clapham and Streatham to Croydon and then due south in a more-or-less straight line (much as it does today) as far as the northern outskirts of Brighton.

In those far-off days Brighton was growing fast, and a railway serving it was an obvious project, but Rennie's ambitious proposal did nothing beyond provoking opposing schemes, which were mutually destructive. In 1836 there were more than a dozen routes for Parliament to choose from. The list was soon reduced to two, by Rennie and Robert Stephenson — of which Rennie's, being the first, took much the shorter route and was thus considered the more suitable. But although Stephenson's line was 8 miles longer it was better with regard to locomotive hauling power, as the gradients were much

easier. After much effort Rennie secured the support of the people of Brighton, whereas Stephenson, whose route passed through land owned by people of influence, had his scheme resisted with the utmost vigour.

The Brighton's first engineer was William Cubitt, who, on seeing that Rennie would secure a share in the Croydon traffic, promptly encouraged a rival scheme, but the rival Bill fell out on account of a technicality. This Brighton battle had caused quite a stir, but nothing happened in 1836, so Stephenson's Bill was passed by the House of Commons, only to be thrown out by the House of Lords in 1837. Captain Alderson was then appointed by the Parliamentary Committee to enquire urgently into those 'Brighton matters', and in 1837 an Act was finally passed whereby the

company was required to construct the whole of the line from the 'Jolly Sailor' to Redhill … and not only that, for when this section was completed it was required to hand over the southern half of the track to the SER, after which the SER was to pay the London & Brighton company for that part of the line, plus 5 per cent. The sum eventually paid by the SER to the LBR was £340,000.

When the London–Brighton main line opened throughout on 21 September 1841 trains departed London Bridge on London & Greenwich metals, running thus as far as Corbett's Lane, from where they ran on London & Croydon tracks as far as the 'Jolly Sailor'; from here they had their own track until they reached a point 6 miles south of Coulsdon where they joined SER track, and it was not until they left the junction at Redhill that they had any chance of clear running on their own track.

To add to the Brighton's problems there were 'gauge troubles'. Robert Stephenson in planning the Liverpool & Manchester Railway had arranged for a 4ft 8½in gauge in his Bill — which did not get passed in Parliament. So to get the next year's Bill through, Sir John Rennie was made engineer in his place. But Rennie, motivated by his extreme dislike of Stephenson, decided upon a gauge of his own, just as I. K. Brunel had found plausible reasons for his width of 7ft 0¼in. So Rennie proved to the satisfaction of all who believed in him that the right gauge to use was 5ft 6in!

Rennie began to lay tracks on the Liverpool & Manchester line

'Surrey, Sussex and so on railway', with exactly the same directorate as the first, became the London & Brighton Railway, with branches to Lewes, Newhaven and Shoreham.

Instead of beginning at Kennington Common (nowadays Kennington Park), as originally proposed by Rennie, the line had to start from the 'Jolly Sailor' public house — next to the site of today's Norwood Junction station, on the London & Croydon Railway. In conjunction with this the LCR had to buy up the extension of the old Surrey Iron Railway, known as the

Croydon, Merstham and Godstone Iron Railway, which ran south from Croydon through Purley along Smitham Bottom Lane.

Further trouble lay ahead for the London & Brighton company, this time thanks to the South Eastern Railway. Having obtained its Act of Parliament of 1836, the SER was empowered to lay its track from Dover through the Weld of Kent to Tonbridge and on to Redstone Hill (now known as Redhill), thereby giving it a link with London. So far, so good — for the SER, at least. However, the London & Brighton

On 21 September 1841 trains departed over the London–Brighton main line over London & Greenwich metals as far as Corbett's Lane, from where they ran on London & Croydon tracks as far as the 'Jolly Sailor' on to Brighton. This view of London Bridge Terminal shows Stroudley tanks left and right, before the days of electrification had taken hold. (John Scott-Morgan)

to his own gauge, but his reign did not last long, and Robert Stephenson resumed his original position and promptly abolished 'Rennie's gauge' in favour of his own — 4ft 8½in. The point was that Robert Stephenson in planning his proposed line to Brighton of course adopted the 4ft 8½in gauge. But what Rennie did not want to acknowledge was that, by choosing to adopt a gauge of his own in order to differ it from the standard gauge of the colliery lines set up by Stephenson, that there would be a conflict, as his trains were to run on London & Greenwich tracks and also on the London & Croydon tracks. It was different from the Stephenson gauge and that was all he wanted. The gauge Rennie wanted for the Brighton was only ½in broader, at 4ft 9in, although it was John Urpeth Rastrick who actually carried out the work. But the SER did not approve of this new

gauge with the extra 'half-inch', as its own tracks had to be to the Stephenson gauge *en route* to Dover, so the Brighton-line trains, which were of standard gauge, ran easily from the 'Jolly Sailor' to Coulsdon and from Redhill on to the south. This remained the situation until the amalgamation of all of the lines to form the LBSCR, when the 'Jolly Sailor' station was moved on a bit to become Norwood Junction — but in the meantime there is another story to tell!

Atmospheric railways

In 1810 George Medhurst, a most ingenious man of whom few have heard, proposed that all letters and parcels should be conveyed through tunnels by means of compressed air. In one of his ideas he described an 'air-tight tunnel' with carriages on rails within it, driven either by

compressed air or sucked through the tunnel by a vacuum patented by a man called Vallance. Another idea was using a smaller tunnel/tube, with a 'piston-carriage' attached by a rod passing along it via a longitudinal valve to a full-sized carriage running over or alongside it in the open air, this system was patented by one Henry Pinkus. The two systems were given a fair showing, but Vallance's system was ridiculed for his 'suffocation scheme', whereas Pinkus's 'Pneumatic Railway System' was tried out near the Kensington Canal, but was never heard of again.

Experiments resumed in 1840, when engineer Samuel Clegg and shipbuilder Joseph Samunda brought out their Atmospheric Railway project. Clegg invented the valve, and Samunda built the plant and found the money. In June of the same year on a temporary part of the unfinished West London Railway, near Wormwood Scrubs, a tube of 9in diameter was laid for another 'Pneumatic Railway System'. The running track was of old contractors rails which were very badly laid — and which, it is interesting to note, had formed part of the original Liverpool & Manchester Railway line. On an incline of about 1 in 120 a maximum speed of 30mph was attained with a load of 5 tons, and 22mph was measured with a load of 11 tons.

So successful were these experiments that directors of other railway companies conducted their own tests. I. K. Brunel went to Dublin to see this new system at work and was so impressed that he started to build the South Devon Railway with this new system.

The atmospheric railway used air pressure to move its trains. Steam engines were used to suck air out of the pipe in front of a train. Air then rushed through the pipe from behind, pushing the train along. In September 1845 an atmospheric train of six carriages was claimed to have reached the (at that time) incredible speed of 70mph.

In 1845 the London & Croydon Railway adopted the atmospheric system for its line between Forest Hill and West Croydon. The system employed 15in pipes laid on the east side of the line — this despite the fact that the Brighton line joined from the east on the approach to East Croydon. The Brighton line therefore had to be crossed by a curious obliquely angled bridge, the slopes of which were 1 in 50, and the 'flying leap', as it was called, was taken by 'the atmospheres' without lessening speed; indeed they travelled at 30mph, and some

were said to have attained speeds as high as 60mph.

The Croydon's vacuum pipe was 5 miles long and ran alongside the existing steam railway track. It was built in two sections, from Forest Hill to Norwood Junction and from Norwood to Croydon. Three steam engines were built at Croydon, Norwood and Forest Hill to provide the power.

Between February and June 1846 an average of 81,000 passengers per month were travelling on this atmospheric railway. One part of the pneumatic infrastructure was the viaduct from Sydenham to Crystal Palace, crossing the main lines. The pneumatic pipe could not cross the metals, so it was necessary to build a flyover and is reputed to be the first of its kind in the world.

The system often broke down. The problems really came along when the sun melted the 'tallow & wax' seal that kept the valve airtight in the vacuum tubes and try as the inventors could, they could not come up with a suitable answer and so the valves began to wear out and together with rats eating the leather and tallow, air would leak out even in cold weather.

In July 1846, the year that the Croydon Atmospheric Railway system was abandoned, the London & Croydon Railway and

the London & Brighton Railway amalgamated to form the London, Brighton & South Coast Railway (LBSCR). By then the South Coast lines had been extended to Hastings in one direction and Chichester in the other. In December of the same year the Newhaven branch had been opened, and the Brighton started its 'cross-Channel' work, the journey from London to Paris taking 12 hours.

A section of pipe from the London & Croydon's atmospheric railway is on loan from the National Railway Museum, York, and is on display at the Museum of Croydon.

During the nineteenth century Penge was administered as a detached hamlet of the parish of Battersea, and this continued right through until 1899, after which Penge Urban District Council was formed, and in 1900 Penge was transferred from the county of Surrey to the county of Kent; later, in 1965, it became part of the London Borough of Bromley. Despite its proximity to London it was entirely rural in character until the march of the railway across the landscape; thereafter its population rapidly grew from just about 1,000 to 13,000, and the area was soon covered by suburban sprawl, although a haven of tranquillity was retained, this

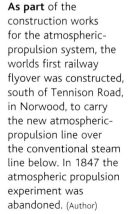

This image from 'The Pictorial Times' of 1846, shows the guard of an Atmospheric Train, operating the brake handle to slow the train down. Between the wheels and the track can be seen the cast-iron pipe which contained the piston, which moved the train. (Author)

As part of the construction works for the atmospheric-propulsion system, the worlds first railway flyover was constructed, south of Tennison Road, in Norwood, to carry the new atmospheric-propulsion line over the conventional steam line below. In 1847 the atmospheric propulsion experiment was abandoned. (Author)

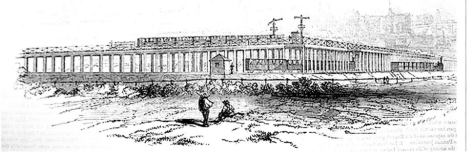

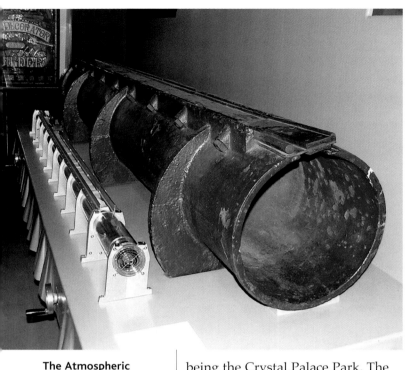

The Atmospheric Railway pipe was 5 miles long and ran alongside the existing steam railway track. This part of the original pipe is on display at the Croydon Museum and is on loan from the National Railway Museum, York. (Author)

The Kearney High-Speed Tube was an untried and untested technology and no one was prepared to run the risk of adopting this system. None of Kearney's schemes ever made it past the drawing board and the Kearney Tube idea faded away. The prototype system was tried out at Crystal Palace Park in 1911. (Author)

being the Crystal Palace Park. The character of the upper part of Penge was fundamentally altered again by the decision to re-erect the Crystal Palace from Hyde Park on this hilltop. Over the years the area has been served by various forms of transport, including the Croydon Canal (from 1809 to 1836) and six types of rail traction — conventional steam (1839-1928), atmospheric (1845/6), pneumatic (1864, for 600yd near the eastern corner of the park), Kearney's High-Speed Tube monorail (1911), overhead electric (1911-28) and third-rail electric (from 1928). On the roads, in addition to horse-drawn vehicles there were electric trams (1906-36) and trolleybuses (1936-59) as well as motor vehicles, which were ably served by a nineteenth-century petrol station.

The Crystal Palace Pneumatic Railway — sometimes referred to

as an atmospheric railway — was built and was operational within a matter of months in 1864, at the lower end of Crystal Palace Park. In contrast with the earlier atmospheric design there was no awkward little pipe with its 'difficult-to-maintain valve seal'. Instead, the whole carriage was put inside the giant vacuum tube with a collar of bristles at its end kept the seal tight. It was successful enough to encourage the construction of a longer, more serious project, the Waterloo & Whitehall Pneumatic Railway, although the Whitehall project would never be completed, as a recession and a banking crisis

meant that funding ran out. The Crystal Palace Pneumatic Railway ran for 600yd in a 10ft-diameter brick tunnel between Penge and Sydenham gates in Crystal Palace Park. The tunnel — although most of it was above ground and covered with soil to give it a 'dug-out' tunnel appearance — had a gradient of 1 in 15, and the railway went round in a sharp curve. It had a coach which could seat 35 people and had a sliding door at each end. There was a remote steam engine coupled to a fan located at the southern end near to the boathouse, which provided the required vacuum. The collar of bristles that

FIG. 41.—The Car is 45 ft. long, and equipped with two motors of 50 h.p. each. The Car seats forty-six persons.

FIG. 42.—Kearney's High-Speed Railway, showing method of construction for Surface Railways.

The Crystal Palace Pneumatic Railway - also known as the Crystal Palace Atmospheric Railway, was constructed near Crystal Palace in south London, at around 1864 by Thomas Webster Rammell and was one of the tourist attractions featured at the Crystal Palace exhibition site. It was the second close encounter of a pneumatic railway with the LBSCR. Power to the novelty ride was provided by a large fan of 22 feet diameter, that was powered by a steam engine. On the return journeys, the fan was reversed to create a vacuum to suck the carriage backwards, whilst the carriage used its brakes to come to a stop. Although not positively known, it is believed that a GWR locomotive of 7ft ¼in Broad-Gauge was used to create the vacuum to operate the system and that the single coach used, may well have been a converted GWR coach. Remnants of the tunnel were found in 1992 in Crystal Palace Gardens. The Penge area was considerably altered by the decision to re-erect the 'Crystal Palace' from Hyde Park in this area and of the LBSCR to build a railway line to serve this great tourist attraction. (Author)

The Crystal Palace Atmospheric Railway, was constructed in Crystal Palace Park and ran between Anerley and Sydenham gates, at around 1864. This is the scene today looking at the same location, as compared to that of the previous image. (Author)

made it airtight enabled the coach to be sucked or pushed along, at a speed of about 25mph, the 600yd journey taking about 50 seconds to complete. (The rumour persists that the railway tunnel, along with the carriage, was simply bricked up and still remains below ground, although recent excavation has revealed little more than what would appear to be a sleeper.)

After the original Crystal Palace of 1851, built by Sir Joseph Paxton in Hyde Park, had been dismantled, the structure was rebuilt in a modified and enlarged form on Penge Common next to Sydenham Hill, an affluent South London suburb full of large villas. It stood there from 1854 until its destruction by fire in 1936. The new exhibition was opened by Queen Victoria on 10 June 1854, and on the same day the branch line to it opened from Sydenham and began services which were

This early view of Anerley Station is viewed from the north east, looking towards the south west and shows a view of the second Crystal Palace - the first having been at Hyde Park. At the front is a train of four-wheeled coaches which is just entering Anerley Station. (Author)

then the only means of access to the exhibition site. The extension of that branch to New Wandsworth opened on 1 December 1856.

The Grosvenor Canal and the development of a London terminus

During the summer of 1857 a scheme was mooted for an independent Grosvenor Basin terminus in the West End of London, 'for the use of the Southern Railways of England'. The station here was originally referred to as the Grosvenor Terminus, but it was later renamed Victoria Station, being sited at the end of Victoria Street. Around this time there were three other railway companies that were also seeking to build a railway terminus in Westminster — the Great Western, the London & North Western and the East Kent, although the first two already had rail access to Battersea through their joint ownership (with the LBSCR) of the West London line. In 1858 the East Kent Railway (EKR) leased the remaining lines of the West End of London & Crystal Palace Railway (WELCPR) from Shortlands station and also negotiated temporary running powers over the lines recently acquired by the LBSCR, pending the construction of its own line into west London. On 23 July 1859 these four companies together formed the Victoria Station & Pimlico Railway Co (VSPR), with the object of extending the railway from Stewarts Lane Junction, Battersea across the River Thames to a more convenient location nearer the West End, and the following month the EKR changed its name to the London, Chatham & Dover Railway.

On the north side of the River Thames the new line followed part of the route of the Grosvenor Canal, with Victoria station being built on part of the former canal basin site. Victoria Station required the construction of a new bridge of mixed gauge — standard gauge and also broad gauge to cater for the GWR's trains, over the River Thames. The bridge, originally known as Victoria Bridge, later became known as Grosvenor Bridge.

The LBSCR had hoped to amalgamate with the VSPR and in 1860 introduced a Parliamentary Bill that would have allowed it to do so, but this was opposed by the GWR and the LCDR and rejected. As a compromise the LBSCR was permitted to lease Victoria station from the VSPR, agreeing to accommodate the other railways until a terminus could be built for them all on an adjoining site.

Lines opened from the south opened as far as Battersea on 29 March 1858 and subsequently were extended to Battersea Pier on the banks of the River Thames. A passenger station similar to that at New Wandsworth was built,

The Act of Parliament that gave authority for Crystal Palace to be built in Hyde Park, contained a condition that it should be removed when the show was over. Joseph Paxton its designer secured a temporary reprieve and there were plans for it to go to Battersea Park and Kew Gardens, but eventually it was sent to Crystal Palace Park, where the structure was re-erected and enlarged. On the evening of 30 November 1936, fire consumed the Crystal Palace, with the efforts of eighty nine fire-engines and 438 firemen proving to be futile. The wooden floors, furniture, fitments and orchestra all burned, the glass melted and the iron buckled. It was said that as many as 500,000 people gathered to watch the demise of the fairy tale palace and many wept openly. The author visited the remains of the site some forty years ago and to his amazement, there, hidden in the bushes were still parts of the cast iron ornamentation finials that topped part of the iron work of the second Crystal Palace. The casting that the author found is seen here and dates back to 1851, which in 2017 made it 166 years old! (Author)

although this no longer exists. Two years later the railway finally reached its objective at Pimlico. The station, which was located immediately to the north of Victoria Railway Bridge was called Grosvenor Road station. Shortly afterwards the railway tracks were extended to Victoria.

The Grosvenor Canal left the River Thames east of Chelsea Bridge and ran for half a mile northwards to a basin the size of which was described in 1878 as 'immense'. The canal as originally built had extended an existing creek and was navigable around 1824. It earned its keep by carrying coal and stone inwards from the River Thames. The canal was progressively shortened, first when the Grosvenor Basin disappeared under the building of the new Victoria Station on the western side and which would become known as the Brighton side and which was built around 1858. The VSPR obtained an Act of Parliament, which ratified an agreement between them and the Duke of Westminster, allowing the station to be built on the basin site and a new towpath was to be constructed between Ebury Bridge and Eccleston Bridge, which interestingly enough, is still there

in use today by railway staff. The new Victoria Station opened on 1 October 1860.

As the railway continued to expand, more room was needed, and another Act of Parliament was obtained by the LBSCR in 1899 which allowed the canal above Ebury Bridge to be closed. This took effect c.1902, the canal being reduced to around half its original length. It was shortened again when the Ebury Bridge Housing Estate was built in the 1930s over part of the canal route. A bricked-up arch of Ebury Bridge, located adjacent to the Ebury Bridge Housing Estate, shows where part of the canal's route originally ran. So, during the process of building Victoria Station and the Ebury Bridge Housing Estate, the canal was shortened to finally becoming a dock at Gatliff Road. Following the cutback of the canal to this point, the Duke of Westminster sold what was left of the canal to Westminster City Council and its primary function became rubbish removal. Barges entering the dock from the River Thames under Grosvenor Road by Chelsea Bridge, were then loaded with rubbish and were taken to the Essex Marshes on behalf of Westminster City Council. At its

Victoria Bridge, was the first railway bridge to cross the River Thames in the London area. It began its life as a mixed gauge two-track railway bridge designed by Sir John Fowler. It carried Great Western Railway broad-gauge trains, London Brighton and South Coast trains and London Chatham and Dover trains, all into Victoria Station. The bridge's four river arches were of wrought iron segments. At the north and south ends were wrought iron plate girder land spans. In 1865, work commenced on a new structure immediately adjacent to the east - downriver side of Fowler's original bridge. Designed by Sir Charles Fox & Son, it increased the number of available tracks to seven. The new section was also made of wrought iron and it repeated the elevation profile of its neighbour.
The same formula, this time using steel, was again followed for further widening in the early 20th century, this time on the west side and this brought two more tracks into service in 1907. By the mid-20th century, the older structures were deteriorating and carrying much heavier loads than they were designed for. The replacement rail bridge - the present Grosvenor Bridge, was built in phases, beginning in 1963. (Author)

The then - newfangled 'pneumatic railway', had a number of close encounters with the 'Brighton Line' and one was located at a site in 1861 which was set immediately in front of where Battersea Power Station is set today. Thomas Webster Rammell came up with the idea for the pneumatic railway and his greatest success was the London Pneumatic Dispatch Company, a predecessor of the more famous Post Office Railway that still lies under London. To test the system, Thomas Rammell and Josiah Clark set up a length of tube just over 450 yards in length in Battersea Park during 1861. In this view, Victoria Railway Bridge, constructed in 1860 by the Victoria Station and Pimlico Railway to carry trains into Victoria Station, can be seen, with one of the towers of the first Chelsea Bridge behind that. The pneumatic railway trial was successful and it wasn't such a big leap to scale up the pneumatic tube to carrying passengers and that is what they did next, at probably the most famous example of such a railway, down at Crystal Palace, which was the location for another close encounter with the LBSCR trains. (Author)

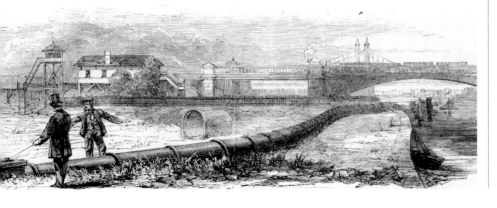

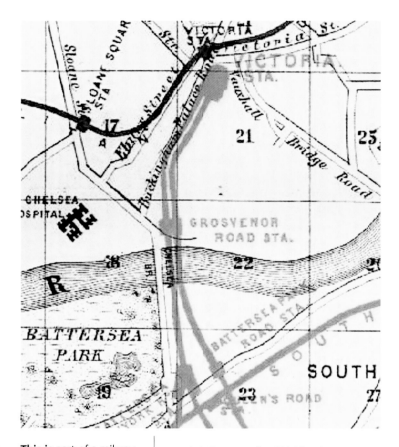

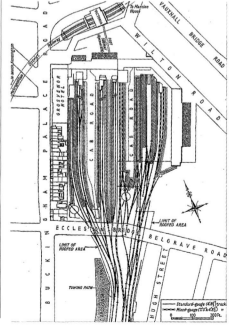

This is part of a railway map of 1889, showing the position of Grosvenor Road Station. Located on the north bank of the River Thames and located opposite Battersea Power Station - although obviously the power station was not built until many years later. Grosvenor Road Station originally had platforms and station buildings belonging exclusively to the LBSCR which were on the western side of the line between 1870 - 1907, while the LCDR side platforms were on the eastern side and they were there between 1867 - 1911. (Author)

The Grosvenor Canal was a canal located in the Pimlico area of London and it opened in 1825. The canal basin which was located at the north end of the canal was progressively drained and Victoria Station and its track work was built on this site. Gradually the canal was shortened as land was reclaimed slowly for the railway tracks to be built into Victoria Station. Finally, the Ebury Bridge Housing Estate was built over the remains, leaving just a small section of canal that was used for refuse barge traffic. Here are the remains of the bricked-up arch located passing under Ebury Bridge, as seen from the Ebury Bridge Housing Estate side. (Author)

This early map pre-dates the rebuilding of the London, Brighton and South Coast Railway - LBSCR station, with its additional train shed south of Eccleston Bridge occupying the site of the canal. The site on the western side was restricted due to housing on Buckingham Palace Road and the location of the Grosvenor Canal pinched the 'throat' of the station. At this time the London, Chatham and Dover Railway, had its entrance on the east of the station located in Hudson Place. The Metropolitan District Railway on the north of the station, had a foot subway linking it to the main station that was opened in 1878. (Author)

This relic from the past is located at 123A Grosvenor Road. Located on the north bank of the River Thames, it originally formed part of Grosvenor Road Station, which had platforms and station buildings belonging to the LBSCR and the LCDR. This building is Grade II listed and was used to collect tickets from passengers travelling to Victoria Station. (Author)

peak, 8,000 tons of refuse were loaded onto barges each week and it remained in use until 1995, making it the last canal in London to operate commercially. A small part of it remains among the Grosvenor Waterside development. The lock and the basin between it and the River Thames have been retained, as has some of the upper basin. The lock has three sets of gates, two facing away from the Thames and a third set facing towards the River Thames, to cope with high tides, where the river level exceeds that in the canal. The third set was first fitted some time between 1896 and 1916.

Grosvenor Road Station has now gone, although one of the station buildings survives, like many other stations and their names, which were mostly named after local public houses: 'Dartmouth Arms' became Forest Hill; 'Jolly Sailor' became Norwood Junction; Godstone Road became Caterham Junction and is now known as Purley, Greyhound Lane — named after the 'Greyhound' public house located on a lane of the same name, located on the line from Croydon to Balham — opened in 1892, has become Streatham Common and quite a number of stations have been absorbed in new ones, the last and largest being Victoria.

More than 115 million people pass through it each year, but Victoria Station in its current form has grown from the merging of two stations.

Marsh Atlantic
Locomotive number 38, awaits departure from Brighton with an express service, c.1910. (John Scott-Morgan)

The London, Chatham & Dover Railway station was opened on 25 August 1862, the SECR station's new frontage being completed in 1908. The train-shed was designed by Sir John Fowler, Consultant Engineer to the VSPR. It has a segmental tied arch roof with light iron tie-rods arranged polygonally between radial iron struts. It comprises two spans, the first of which measures 127ft by 455ft, the other 129ft by 385ft. The building frontage was designed by

A. W. Blomfield, architect to the SECR, and is in Portland stone. It incorporates four caryatids supporting two broken pediments.

The original LBSCR station was designed by Robert Jacomb-Hood and opened on 1 October 1860. Demolished early in 1906 and reopened in rebuilt form in June of that year, it was significantly shortened during redevelopment work in 1979. In common with the frontage, the train-shed was designed by Sir Charles Morgan,

the LBSCR's Chief Engineer. Of transverse ridge-and-furrow construction, it was covered by a longitudinal ridge-and-furrow roof. The station frontage was built in red brick and Portland stone in the Edwardian Baroque style.

Designed by J. T. Knowles in Italianate style with a French Renaissance roof, the Grosvenor Hotel, which dominates the station, opened in 1861 and was purchased by LBSCR in 1899. Leased to Gordon Hotels and reopened on

The triangle of land that formed the station yard at Grosvenor Terminus at Victoria, was the gathering point for many horse-drawn cabs and coaches in the 1890s. The fenced-off yard was formally named Terminus Place and the area was then taken over by buses to become Victoria Bus Station. This image full of detail, shows many Hansom Cabs waiting for trade and on the right can be seen signs advertising trains to the City by the District Railway. The castle looking building in the top left is the Grosvenor Hotel , which is located adjacent to the Brighton side of the Terminus and was completed in 1861 in the Second Empire style. As part of the LBSCR station rebuild, it was extended over the railway company's new frontage and has 357 bedrooms. On the left are many signs advertising many exotic places, including Germany and Crystal Place. (Author)

A clear view of Victoria Station with a canopy at the front and which still survives. Note the station forecourt full of hansom cabs. (John Scott-Morgan)

10 December 1900, it was extended in 1907, Morgan designing a new frontage for the station beneath. British Transport Hotels took over in 1977, and in 1983 it was sold to Thistle Hotels.

The two stations were unified in 1923, following the Grouping, and the eastern platforms were extended in 1960. A British United Airways terminal was operational by 1 May 1962, the BOAC terminal following suit a year later. The south central concourse was enlarged in 1979, with the Gatwick Rail-Air reception opening in 1980.

The Brighton side of Victoria Station as seen in Edwardian times. As ever the statutory W. H. Smiths Bookstall is present. (Author)

In 1865 Victoria Station became the scene of an interesting social experiment that enabled workmen to travel on two trains each day - either on their way to work or on their way home. The cost of this new form of transport was at the special weekly ticket rate of one shilling. This early form of travel transformed the lives for many people as a necessity to earn their daily wage. (Author)

A view of Victoria Station's roof in all of its glory which was designed by Sir Charles Morgan, chief engineer for the LBSCR. It was 'transverse ridge and furrow' in construction, covered by a longitudinal ridge and furrow roof. This magnificent structure was demolished when the station was redeveloped internally in the 1980's, with the addition of shops within the concourse and above the Brighton side platforms as the "Victoria Place" shopping centre and became a soul-less shopping and office complex. In his youth, the author lived nearby and frequently walked beneath this magnificent structure, exiting the station up the cab rank road seen in the centre. (Author)

Electrification

The LBSCR opened its electrified South London line on 1 December 1909, using an overhead high-tension single-phase system. Other routes followed, and 12 May 1911 saw the opening of the route from Victoria to Crystal Palace via Balham and West Norwood. Within a few years the line from Victoria to Selhurst Station was also converted, and in 1920 that from London Bridge to South Croydon was completed. In 1921 plans were drawn up for an extension of overhead electrification to Brighton, but the 1923 Grouping intervened and it only reached Coulsdon North, before the Southern Railway decided to standardise the electric power system using the 'third-rail' system of the former London & South Western Railway. In 1928/9 the existing overhead power lines were removed and the system was converted to third-rail operation.

The decision to electrify the entire Brighton main line was taken in 1929, and the section from Coulsdon North to Three Bridges was opened in July 1932. The section from Three Bridges to Brighton and (and west as far as West Worthing) was operational from 1 January 1933.

The Crystal Palace electric stock units, were built in 1911 - 1913, to provide the trains required for the LBSCR's AC overhead electrification to Crystal Palace and the surrounding area. This stock comprised of ninety cars, which were used in three-car formations. Here one of the units is seen emerging from Crystal Palace Tunnel into Crystal Palace Station. (Author)

This fascinating view shows a different era at Victoria Station. A Crystal Palace Line train waits in Platform 2 ready for departure. After 1923, and the amalgamation of the LBSC & SECR, the Brighton Line platforms were renumbered and so Platform 2, became the Platform 10 of today. The image shows at the head of the formation a Motor Coach driving end sporting head code '1' which for AC Overhead System Headcodes used circa 1911 to 1929 indicated a Victoria - Crystal Palace service running via Streatham Hill. (John Scott-Morgan)

On 17 June 1928 standard 3SUB sets replaced the 'Elevated Electric' AC sets on the South London Line and so brought down the curtain on the LBSC's pioneering London suburban electrification system. The sixteen driving motor cars were taken away into the works and were converted to use the third rail system. Eight of them were fitted with new traction motors and other electrical equipment, with the others converted to become driving trailers. Upon completion they were numbered 1801-08 in April 1934. They then returned to service and worked the South London Line until they were replaced by BR Standard 2EPB units in the 1950s. Here unit Nº 1805 is seen working a Victoria - London Bridge via South London Line service at Wandsworth Road. Notice the school boy trainspotters at the end of the platform. (John Scott-Morgan)

For the opening of their 'Elevated Electric railway' the LBSC introduced 8 three-car sets. Each set comprising of 2 Driving Motor Brake Third (DMBT) cars formed either side of a Trailer First. This was the first departure from second class by the Company and resulted in an over-optimistic number of first class seats, 56 against 132 thirds. Here DMBT Nº 3204 is seen with a Driving Trailer Composite (DTC). The DTC was an acknowledgement that the original first class seating idea was extreme, as it had reduced first class accommodation to just 16 seats along with 60 third class seats. The DMBT carries a 'SL' headcode designating Victoria - London Bridge via the South London Line. The picture is dated post 1925, as from 1925, previously no headcode was carried for this service. (John Scott-Morgan)

The overhead electrification of the Coulson & Wallington lines - although well advanced, was not completed until after the LBSC was merged into the Southern Railway in 1923. Delivered in 1926, some of the vehicles appeared in LBSC umber livery while later deliveries were in standard SR green. Shown here is a Driving Motor Luggage Van (DMLV) generally referred to as a '*milk-van*'. These vehicles were actually electric locomotives and 21 vehicles were delivered numbered 10101-10121. (John Scott-Morgan)

For the 1935 electrification of the lines to Eastbourne and Hastings seventeen more six-car sets were introduced. Designated as 6PAN sets, the units were a development of the 6PUL but had a First Class trailer with a pantry serving light refreshments in place of the Pullman car. Here unit N° 3029 is seen waiting to depart from London Bridge for Brighton. The Trailer Buffet Kitchen First (Lav) otherwise known as the 'pantry' is the third vehicle in the formation. (John Scott-Morgan)

This view at the Brighton side of Victoria Station shows on the left a 'Brighton Line' built 6PAN unit Nº 3023 sporting a '52' headcode for a Victoria - Ore via Quarry Line and Eastbourne service, with on the right, a former 'Kent Coast' 4CEP formation having just arrived, with the head code panel still showing red. Similar to the 6PAN, the 4CEP due to changing demands, had been transferred over from its former line to work elsewhere. (John Scott-Morgan)

A view from Ebury Bridge of the steep Grosvenor Bank incline met by trains almost immediately after departing from Victoria Station, London. The climb takes them past the Grosvenor Depot on the left and up to Grosvenor Bridge, across the River Thames on their way south, passing the former Battersea Power Station. The former Grosvenor Canal used to run behind the wall on the right. The remaining stub of the Grosvenor Canal joins the River Thames at a point between the edge of the trees and the tall speckled building on the right. (Author)

A remnant from the past glories of the former LBSCR, can still be seen at Victoria Station in London. This map shows the system of the network of tracks from London to the south coast. (Author)

Chapter 3

GENESIS OF THE BRIGHTON ATLANTICS

As part of their master-plan the LBSCR's directors developed and expanded their railway system to serve the popular residential areas of South London and Surrey, notably Camberwell, Tooting, Croydon, Banstead and Epsom Downs. By 1869 the plan was starting to work; the railway had a route mileage of some 365 miles, and the money was rolling in, a gross revenue of just over £708,000 being recorded for the second half of 1868. Matters

continued in a similar vein until the end of the Victorian era, by which time the development of electric tramways, particularly within the London area, was beginning to eat seriously into the company's profits. To counteract the problem the LBSCR was galvanised to take drastic action. Thus, following the principle 'if you cant beat 'em, join 'em', it developed the tram-system idea and brought electric traction to its own rails. The company knew that electrification would eventually spread down its main

line to the South Coast and decided to employ a high-tension overhead supply system using a 6,600V alternating current. The result was that in 1909 it inaugurated its famous overhead electrification of the South London suburbs, and thereafter it continued to expand the system until the Grouping in 1923.

The electrification of the LBSCR's suburban system was a triumph — so much so that it became a victim of its own success, overcrowding of trains being a regular feature of railway journeys in South London. However, overhead electrification was regarded by some in authority as being more preferable for longer distances and unsuitable for local commuter services. Eventually the Brighton line was electrified, but with the third-rail system used by the LSWR, and it is this system that remains in use today. Recently, however, there has been talk of re-electrifying the Brighton line using the 25kV AC system, which is commonly used in railway electrification systems worldwide, especially for high-speed rail

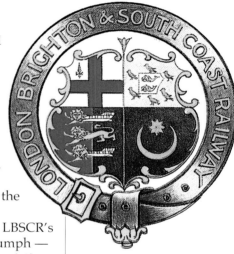

A close up of the coat of arms used by the London, Brighton and South Coast Railway. (Author)

This is one of the the 'Motor Luggage Vans', which were nicknamed 'Milk-Vans', each of which had four 250hp GEC traction motors. They were used on Coulsdon North and Wallington electrified services from London. The stock which was built by the Metropolitan Cammell Carriage and Wagon Company in Birmingham, was in service from 1925-1929. (Author)

Responding to the demands of the day to reduce its operating costs, the LBSCR decided to produce a glorified version of the street tramcar and run it on its rural lines. The new rail motors were cheap to construct, and so the LBSCR decided to give them a go. But compared with operating a street tramcar, rail motors usually required a three-man crew - a driver, a fireman and a guard, which all added to the expense of a service that saw few passengers and which was designed to have low operating costs. The rail motor was deemed to be an economic failure, however, the LBSCR had been seen to demonstrate a willingness to try out new working practices to achieve an efficient and economic railway system. Here is a Stroudley designed 2-4-0 tank locomotive No 82 Boxhill complete with a single coach as would have been used for branch line workings on the LBSCR. (John Scott-Morgan)

When D. E. Marsh became Locomotive Superintendent of the LBSCR, his first two designs were equally as radical as the introduction of the Atlantic express passenger tender locomotives, with two steam railcars and two petrol railcars being produced. Here is petrol Rail Motor N° 3. It ran on the branch line between Brighton and Kemp Town every half hour and had seating accommodation for forty eight passengers. (John Scott-Morgan)

services. So maybe the LBSCR had the idea right all along.

Before electrification took hold the majority of the LBSCR's locomotives were tank engines, and this reflects the type of traffic and service conditions prevailing at this time. Indeed, on passenger services there were about three times as many tanks as tender engines. Tank engines were popular because of the restricted servicing facilities at railway termini, along with the limited time that was available to perform the turning of tender engines. The latter was probably the main reason why tank engines dominated the Brighton line and this would have caused considerable headaches for senior operating managers.

Although the tank engine was useful in terms of achieving "a fast turnaround of service" the LBSCR's Board was far from happy with the performance of its steam locomotives in general, although this seems unlikely to have been any worse on the Brighton than elsewhere. The old-fashioned 'singles' of the day were blamed for poor timings, but the true reason was that excessive loadings were now becoming the norm.

On routes where passenger numbers were light a single coach with its own prime mover was seen as the answer to a railwayman's prayers and the idea was adopted in some areas. Rail motors, as they were known, were not a new idea, however, having been introduced as early as 1848. Although the idea was sound generally, the early designs were unsuccessful technically. But a system that was favourite at this

time, was that of the street tramcar, which had evolved and before long, the customary horse traction had been replaced by small steam locomotives and in many cases tramways soon adopted electric traction.

Responding to the demands of the day and seeking to reduce its operating costs, the LBSCR decided to produce a glorified version of the street tramcar and run it on its rural lines, serving new stopping places, which closely served the new, ever-expanding suburban housing schemes. The new rail motors were cheap to construct, so the LBSCR decided to give them a try. But rail motors did have a number of disadvantages, for example, their frequency of service and the closeness of their stopping places, could not match those of the competing tramcars. Instead of a separate steam engine being provided to move the rail motors, as per the street tramcar, the rail motors had a steam engine actually built inside the very limited space that was available in the coach body, which made them mechanically inefficient. With this system the power was insufficient to handle the hauling of extra vehicles for the carriage of parcels or indeed pulling additional coaches at times of exceptional demand — such as public holidays. Also, compared with the street tramcar, rail motors usually required a three-man crew — a driver, a fireman and a guard, which all added to the expense of a service that was designed to have low operating costs. This all added a significant expense to a service that was designed to have low operating

A nice bright sunny poster showing 'the way ahead' for rail transport on some of the branch line services of the 'Brighton line'. However, it was not to be a success. (Author)

costs. This all added a significant expense to a service which saw few passengers. Although the rail motor was deemed a failure the LBSCR had at least demonstrated a willingness to try out new working practices in its efforts to achieve an efficient and economic railway system.

Over the years the LBSCR engaged a succession of engineers to design locomotives capable of working its increasingly heavily loaded express passenger services. Appointed in 1904, Douglas Earle Marsh had already gained considerable experience and repute, having spent his early career at Swindon Works at the GWR before moving to the GNR at Doncaster, where he became assistant to the remarkable H. A. Ivatt. Such was the urgency for express passenger motive power on the Brighton line that Marsh — with Ivatt's full support — obtained from his former employers a full set of drawings for the large-boilered Atlantic. To these he made a few amendments of his own, the result being the

five 4-4-2 express locomotives of the 'H1' class, built by Kitson's of Leeds between December 1905 and February 1906.

Although built to Marsh's design, the second batch of Brighton-line large-boilered Atlantics — known

as the 'H2' class — were modified by his deputy, Lawson Billinton, who, by then was Acting Chief Mechanical Engineer, Marsh himself being absent on extended sick leave. In 1912, Marsh having resigned, Billinton took over the top

No. 251. LATEST ATLANTIC TYPE EXPRESS LOCOMOTIVE.

Having gained much experience from working at Doncaster Works, D. E. Marsh moved on to Brighton Works. Such was the urgency for express passenger motive power on the Brighton Line, that he obtained a set of drawings from Doncaster Works of the newfangled large boiler Atlantic locomotive. This type of locomotive had already been tested and proven on the GNR to good effect, so he was already onto a winner. The end result was an amazing class of locomotive for the Brighton Line. Here is a contemporary image of the Great Northern Railway's N° 251; the locomotive that D. E. Marsh had helped to develop at Doncaster and upon which his Brighton Atlantic tender locomotives were based. (John Scott-Morgan)

position permanently, holding it until the Grouping in 1923. The six H2 Atlantics were built at Brighton Works and remained on front-line Brighton express duties until the arrival of 'King Arthur' 4-6-0s in 1925.

Marsh's 4-4-2 tank engines were not as successful as the H1s and H2s and fell way short of expectations, the earlier I1s and I2s being disliked by footplate crews on account of their poor steaming qualities. But thanks to improvements suggested by Chief Draughtsman B. K. Field superheating was later introduced,

and this made a noticeable difference on the 'I3' class.

On a network where the longest non-stop run was less than 60 miles it seemed to make sense to use tank engines on the regular express passenger workings, the H1 and H2 Atlantic tender engines being reserved for prestigious workings such as the 'Southern Belle' Pullman. The H1s (Nᵒs 37-41) and H2s (421-6) were taken over by the Southern Railway at the Grouping in 1923, at which time each locomotive was recorded as having a financial value of £3,262. As part of the SR's Publicity Department's

drive to create a better image for travellers on the system the H1s and H2s were named after coastal locations served by the railway. Following the withdrawal in 1940 of the cross-Channel ferry service the locomotives were left with little work to do, so several were placed in store or demoted to lesser duties. Following the end of hostilities the 'H2s' resumed their boat-train duties and (in most cases) continued working until the late 1950s, and it was one of these locomotives, Nᵒ 32424 *Beachy Head*, that became the very last Atlantic to remain in service with British Railways.

The first two types of D. E. Marsh's 4-4-2 tank engines, the I1s & I2s, were disliked by footplate crews due to their poor steaming qualities. However, super-heating improvements from Chief Draughtsman B. K. Field were later introduced and made a noticeable difference, turning the I3s into a much appreciated class of engine. This view shows I1 class 4-4-2T Nᵒ 1 ready to leave the shed for its next turn of duty. (John Scott-Morgan)

One of D. E. Marsh's Atlantic express locomotives which he built for the Brighton Line, H1 class 4-4-2 N° 39, was built by Kitson & Co of Leeds, in January 1906 and lasted until February 1951, having completed 516,774 miles. D. E. Marsh abandoned the Brighton practice of naming locomotives and as a result only one of the H1s bore a name during LBSCR days, N° 39, which was named *La France* in 1913, prior to working the train for the visit of the French President. The name was carried until January 1926, at which time the Southern Railway renamed the locomotive *Hartland Point*. (Author)

One of D. E. Marsh's Atlantic express locomotives which he built for the Brighton Line, H1 class 4-4-2 N° 40, was constructed by Kitson & Co of Leeds, in January 1906. It lasted until December 1957, having completed 1,000,476 miles. (John Scott-Morgan)

H1 class 4-4-2 Nº 41, was built by Kitson & Co of Leeds in January 1906 and lasted until March 1944, having completed 999,944 miles. (John Scott-Morgan)

Chapter 4

DOUGLAS EARLE MARSH

Douglas Earle Marsh was born in Norfolk on 4 January 1862 and interestingly enough was educated at Brighton College, before going to study at University College, London. He was the Locomotive Superintendent of the London, Brighton and South Coast Railway from 1905 to 1912 and was the man who introduced the Atlantic type of locomotive to the Brighton Line. (Author)

Douglas Earle Marsh was Locomotive Superintendent of the London, Brighton & South Coast Railway from 1904 to 1912. Born at Aylsham, Norfolk, on 4 January 1862, Marsh was educated at Brighton College and at University College, London. He began his railway career on the Great Western Railway at Swindon, under William Dean, becoming Assistant Works Manager in 1888, after just eight years. In 1896 he became Chief Assistant Mechanical Engineer of the Great Northern Railway at Doncaster Works, where in 1897 he assisted H. A. Ivatt with the design of the legendary 'Klondike' Atlantics.

When Marsh arrived at Brighton his ideas were considered by some to be different from the usual and lacking a sense of direction. But he had a strong opinion about the colour of his locomotives. He ordered that the colour of his locomotives should be changed from Stroudley's yellow to a dark umber (for passenger locomotives) or plain black (for goods locomotives). In conjunction with this he abolished previously applied names. His first two designs were equally as radical, introducing two steam powered railcars and two petrol-driven railcars.

Marsh started work at Brighton on 23 November 1904, at which time the LBSCR was in urgent need of new large passenger locomotives. As Marsh had been heavily involved with the design of the GNR Atlantics, immediately he assumed office at Brighton Works, he ordered a set of drawings of Doncaster's large-boiler Atlantic locomotive and made a few amendments, such as differences to the footplate undulations, the chimney and the cab which had standard R. J. Billinton fittings. He

also increased the boiler pressure from 175 to 200lb. His modifications were marked on the original Doncaster drawings in red ink and once the amendments were completed, he ordered a batch of five locomotives from Messrs Kitson & Co of Leeds in 1905 and 1906. Employed on the fastest and most prestigious workings between London and the South Coast, these masterpieces of locomotive engineering set new standards of speed and reliability that would not

When D. E. Marsh became Locomotive Superintendent of the LBSCR, his first two designs were equally as radical as the introduction of the Atlantic express passenger tender locomotives, with two steam railcars and two petrol railcars being produced. Here is steam Rail Motor Nº 1. (John Scott-Morgan)

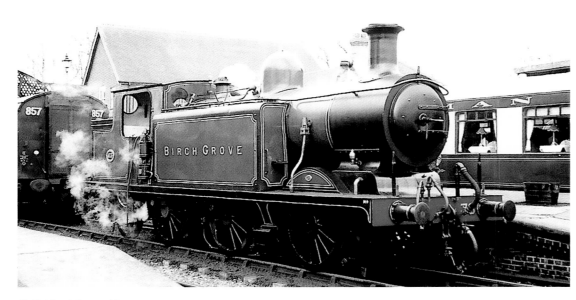

When D. E. Marsh became Locomotive Superintendent of the LBSCR, he did away with William Stroudley's "improved green" livery on his steam locomotives and replaced it with umber livery - the very same colour as used on Pullman cars, such as the one seen on the right here, although they should both be the same shade - there appears to be a difference between the shade. No 473, was one of the last survivors of its class in 1963 and was purchased by a group of preservationists, who took it to the Bluebell Railway in Sussex. Following its long overhaul, No 473, returned to traffic in 1997, to celebrate it's centenary in 1998. Painted in D. E. Marsh's umber livery, it has the name Birch Grove on the side tanks. As was the practice with such Brighton engines, it was named after a town or village in the LBSCR's area. Birch Grove is a small hamlet, just north of Horsted Keynes, and one of its residents, former Prime Minister Harold Macmillan, would have used Horsted Keynes as his local station. (Author)

D. E. Marsh began his railway career at Swindon Works and later, in 1896, he became the Chief Assistant Mechanical Engineer of the Great Northern Railway at Doncaster Works. Here, he assisted H. A. Ivatt, in producing the design of the legendary 4-4-2 Klondike Atlantic type of locomotive - which was named after the Klondike Gold Rush in America, in 1897. Here is an example of that type of locomotive, Nº 983, which was completed in April 1900 and withdrawn on 18 April 1936. (Author)

Douglas Earle Marsh's locomotive classes included two designs of Atlantic 4-4-2 type locomotives, which were heavily based on the GNR designed large-boiler version: the H1 class and H2 class. Here is an example of a GNR large boiler version, Nº 1403, hauling an East Coast Express, c.1910. (John Scott-Morgan)

When completed and delivered, the second batch of the LBSCR's Atlantic tender express locomotives assumed the H2 class identity. This image shows one of D. E. Marsh's magnificent H2 class Atlantic tender express locomotives, which in LBSCR days was the only one fitted with vacuum brake gearing, seen here at Lewes. (John Scott-Morgan)

Wilhelm Schmidt, known as "Hot Steam Schmidt", 1858 - 1924, was a German engineer and inventor. He was the man who achieved the breakthrough in the development of superheated steam technology for steam engines. In 1907, D. E. Marsh's chief draughtsman Basil K. Field persuaded Marsh to fit a Schmidt superheater to one of his 4-4-2 tank locomotive designs - the I3 class. With immediate effect, D. E. Marsh's I3 tank locomotive registered a twenty five per cent decrease in coal consumption. This more or less assured the acceptance of superheating in Britain. Here are drawings - originally published in 1889, showing some of the details of a Schmidt superheater. (Author)

be surpassed until the introduction, decades later, of electric traction.

Another milestone in locomotive design was passed in 1907, when Marsh's chief draughtsman, Basil K. Field, persuaded him to fit a Schmidt superheater system to his 4-4-2 tank-engine design and so created the I3 class. At this time only the Lancashire & Yorkshire Railway had taken the route in Britain to fit superheating systems to its locomotives, but the results were not particularly encouraging. However, as soon as they were released into traffic the superheater-fitted I3s registered a 25 per cent reduction in coal consumption. One was tried out on the London & North Western Railway and ran for 90 miles without taking water. The LNWR took notice and was soon fitting its own locomotives with Schmidt-type superheaters, ensuring the acceptance of superheating in Britain.

Following the success of his I3 4-4-2Ts Marsh decided to revise the class specifications to create a larger tank engine that would be capable of working the heaviest expresses between London and Brighton.

The first was N° 325 *Abergavenny*, turned out by Brighton Works in December 1910. Classified J1, it had a 4-6-2 wheel arrangement and incorporated a Schmidt superheater and Stephenson valve gear. Initial modifications to the firebox helped to reduce coal consumption, and it proved to be a very successful design. A second locomotive was ordered in May 1911, but this

would have Walschaerts valve gear. Soon afterwards Marsh went on prolonged sick leave, and all work ceased. It eventually resumed under the direction of his eventual successor, Lawson Billinton, who made detailed design changes before construction of the second locomotive began. Classified J2, N° 326 *Bessborough* was completed in March 1912. This was considered the faster of the two, although both performed very well, being used on the heaviest trains until after the formation of the Southern Railway in January 1923. However, no further examples were built, and the two Pacific tanks were ultimately withdrawn from service by BR in June 1951.

Marsh's least-successful locomotives were his C3 0-6-0 goods engines, intended to replace the smaller R. J. Billinton C2 0-6-0s on the heaviest workings. They did have an effective boiler, but

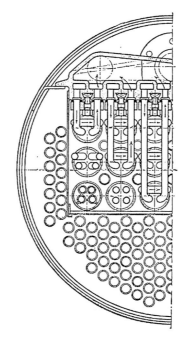

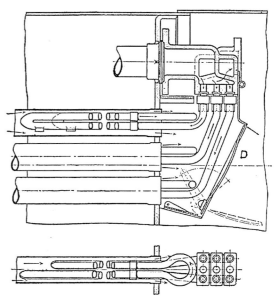

their performance proved to be disappointing, and their coal consumption high, so instead of building further examples Marsh rebuilt the existing members of the C3 class, which spent the rest of their days on secondary goods trains in mid-Sussex. Seven of the class spent most of their time working at Horsham, earning the type the nickname 'Horsham Goods'. The boiler designed by Marsh for his C3 class was later used on the Southern Railway's Z-class 0-8-0s of 1929, with considerably more success. Marsh also rebuilt many of his predecessors' locomotives with larger boilers and so created Classes A1X, B2X, C2X, E4X, E5X and E6X. It was Marsh too who began fitting secondary passenger locomotives with equipment which in cold conditions could be used to feed steam to the rest of the train by means of a through pipe; he thus earned the gratitude of many a commuter who, having endured bitter cold while waiting on the

platform for his or her train, was now revived by the supply of warm air around the feet and legs.

During Marsh's time at Brighton a serious backlog of locomotives awaiting repair built up, to the extent that by 1910 30 per cent of the locomotive stock was unavailable for use. Marsh was blamed for this situation, because of bad planning and organisation because the works were overwhelmed with work. In 1911 matters came to a head. It seems that Marsh was never really popular

with the workforce at Brighton, and following accusations of accounting irregularities (among the more fanciful being that he had pocketed the cost of a locomotive that had never been built) he resigned in July 1911 on the grounds of ill health.

Following his resignation from the LBSCR Marsh became a consulting engineer for the Rio Tinto Zinc Co, in which capacity he continued to work until 1932. He died in Bath on 25 May 1933.

Fitted with a Schmidt superheater, D. E. Marsh's tank locomotives immediately registered a twenty five per cent decrease in coal consumption. One of these locomotives N° 23, was tried out on the London and North Western Railway - LNWR and ran some 90 miles without taking water. The LNWR took notice and were soon fitting its own locomotives with Schmidt superheaters. Here is a works plate from sister I3 class 4-4-2T locomotive N° 85. (Author) (Courtesy of The Brighton Toy & Model Museum, Brighton)

Following the success of his I3 class 4-4-2T locomotives D. E. Marsh decided to enlarge the class specifications to create a tank locomotive capable of hauling the heaviest London to Brighton express trains. The first locomotive - N° 325 was named *Abergavenny* and was classified as J1 class. It incorporated a Schmidt superheater and Stephenson valve gear. It proved to be a successful design and a second locomotive was ordered in May 1911. N° 325 is seen in Southern Railway days sandwiched between L class 4-6-4 tank locomotives otherwise known as Brighton Baltics N° 328 and N° 333 *Remembrance* which was the last new locomotive built by the London, Brighton and South Coast Railway, before it became part of the Southern Railway on 1 January 1923. It was named in honour of the members of the railway killed in the World War I. (John Scott-Morgan)

D. E. Marsh created a second tank locomotive capable of hauling the heaviest London to Brighton express trains. The second locomotive - N° 326, was named *Bessborough* and was classified as J2 class. It incorporated a Schmidt superheater and Walschaerts valve gear. It proved to be a successful design and along with *Abergavenny* survived into British Railways (BR) ownership in 1948. In June 1951 they were both replaced by the new LMS Fairburn designed 2-6-4T locomotives and were withdrawn and scrapped. It is seen at Victoria Station. (John Scott-Morgan)

When completed and delivered, the new batch of the London, Brighton and South Coast Railway's locomotives assumed the identity of H1 class Atlantics. They were a class of steam locomotive with a 4-4-2 wheel arrangement and were constructed for use on express passenger services from London - Brighton. Here is N° 37; the first of the class and completed in December 1905. It survived until July 1951. (John Scott-Morgan)

Chapter 5

THE GREAT NORTHERN CONNECTION

I n the middle of the nineteenth century it was possible to travel by railway from London to Yorkshire, but the route was long and the traveller had to travel from Euston on routes taking them to such places as Rugby and Derby. Eventually a more direct route was proposed from London, heading directly north and passing through Peterborough, where a loop line would be built to Boston, Lincoln and Doncaster, and there would be branches to Sheffield and Wakefield. The bill was passed by parliament, but the original title, London & York Railway, was dropped, and Great Northern Railway was adopted instead.

Plans were made in December 1848 for an area of King's Cross in London to become established as the GNR's southern terminus. The detailed design was made by Lewis Cubitt, with construction work carried out between 1851 — 1852, on the site of a former smallpox hospital. The main part of the station was opened on 14 October 1852 and replaced the temporary terminus, which had been located at Maiden Lane, which had previously opened on 7 August 1850.

The line north from King's Cross to Peterborough had an initial climb that was considered by some to be severe for its time. It had gradients of around 1 in 110 for some miles, after which, there were very few gradients exceeding 1 in 200 for any great distance.

The earliest locomotives ordered by the GNR were of the usual types built by the usual manufacturers of the time. The good news for the GNR, relative latecomers to the market, was that locomotive designs had evolved improved. Order N° 198, for example, dated 5 February 1847, was for six locomotives, a further 44 being covered by order N° 203, dated on 4 March 1847. These small, primitive machines — which had 5ft 6in driving wheels and boilers pressured at 90lb, were taken into stock between 1847 and 1850. Later Archibald Sturrock, Locomotive Superintendent of the GNR from 1850 until 1866, fitted them with compensating levers, which proved to be of great benefit on the relatively poor and lightly constructed track of the mid-nineteenth century.

Over the years the design of steam locomotives continued to develop, among the more notable express types being Patrick Stirling's 4-2-2 'Singles', with their enormous (8ft-diameter) driving wheels. Built for speed and to handle the continuous gradients on the GNR main line between London and York, they were used to compete against the Midland Railway and the LNWR in the 'Races to the North'. Train weights were ever increasing, and until the end of the nineteenth century trains such as the 'Flying Scotsman' (or 'Special Scotch Express', as it was then officially known) still ran with six-wheel coaches in their formation.

In 1900 came a revolutionary change in terms of passenger comfort with the introduction of two new trains of American design and appearance. Each consisted of eight coaches which were bow-ended, 65ft 6in long and rested on two six-wheeled bogies. Restaurant cars were also included in the formation, and the whole train weighed some 265 tons. Similar new coaching stock arrived on other Anglo-Scottish and London–Leeds services, increasing train loads all round. By the turn of the century, however, the Stirling Singles were being taxed as the GNR increased train loadings to match its rivals

Seeking greater power and adhesion for his top-link express locomotives, H. A. Ivatt, with inspiration borrowed from the Baldwin Locomotive Works' design for the Atlantic Coast Line in North America, took the American route and in 1897 designed the first 4-4-2 or Atlantic type of locomotive to enter service in Great Britain. In 1898, twenty-eight years after Patrick Stirling's first 4-2-2 had appeared from Doncaster Works, Britain's first 4-4-2 Atlantic locomotive, N° 990, was ready for work. It is seen here with an extended smokebox at the old York Station, which was set within the city's ancient walls. (Roland Kennington)

on the West Coast main line. Stirling died in office aged 75, and Ivatt took on the daunting task of replacing him as the head of the GNR's locomotive department.

In developing his locomotives Ivatt took another step to improve their water-boiling ability, with sensational results. Seeking greater power and adhesion, he followed the American approach, and in 1897, taking his inspiration from the Baldwin Locomotive Works design for the Atlantic Coast Line in the USA, he designed the first 4-4-2 (Atlantic) locomotive to enter service in Great Britain. In 1898, 28 years after Stirling's first Single had emerged from Doncaster Works, Britain's first Atlantic, N° 990, was ready for work.

Surprisingly the new design of locomotive, instead of being

provided with an enlarged set of cylinders (the maximum dimensions seen thus far being the 19½x28in of the Stirling Singles), featured cylinders of 18½in diameter and 24in stroke. However, instead of a boiler with a heating surface of no more than 1,032sq ft and a fire-gate area of 20ft (as with the Stirling locomotives) the new 4-2-2 had an increased heating surface of 1,442ft and a fire-gate area of 26.8ft. This odd combination saw the Ivatt Atlantics recorded as having a nominal tractive effort of 15,860lb, whereas that of Stirling's last 4-2-2s was 16,100lb. But the tractive-force formula means nothing unless there is sufficient steam to make it effective; Ivatt had publicly proclaimed that in his opinion the capacity of a locomotive was its ability to boil water, and here was

the principal in action. There were no questions as to which actually was the more powerful of the two types: Ivatt's, of course.

Between 1898 and 1903 Doncaster turned out 22 Atlantics, which soon became known as 'Klondikes', this being the time of the Gold Rush in North America. Their design featured a large-capacity boiler, and it was this additional steam-raising capacity that gave them an edge over the Stirling Singles. They were lively locomotives indeed, so much so that Ivatt had to caution his drivers to rein in the speed because stretches of the track between London and Doncaster were considered 'too uneven for safety's sake, with regards to high-speed running'! But the engine-men would have told Ivatt that the cylinders were no match for

H. A. Ivatt's 'Klondike' Nº 3989 is seen working hard leaving a station as the injectors are put on to replenish the boiler with much needed water. Nº 3989, was finished in June 1900 and was the last 'Klondike' to be built. It lasted until April 1938 when it was withdrawn from service and cut-up at Doncaster Works. (Author)

Development of steam locomotives continued with the introduction of large boiler Atlantics. Nº 251 became symbolic of the GNR and this locomotive featured in most of the GNR's advertising and on timetable covers. Large boiler Atlantics proved to be superb locomotives on the East Coast express trains and were the first engines to be built with a wide firebox as a development from the first small boiler Atlantics. (Author)

Large boiler Ivatt Atlantic Nº 1435 was completed in November 1907 and finally withdrawn from service on 20 December 1945 before being cut up at Doncaster Works. Seen here in a contemporary view, it is heading a train of 'heavy Gresley teak bodied passenger coaches. (John Scott-Morgan)

the boiler, and the early Atlantics had to be worked at undesirable and uneconomic rates to achieve the expected performance; in other words, they had to be 'thrashed'.

As ever, the development of steam locomotives continued, now with the introduction of large-boiler Atlantics. They were the first locomotives to be built with a wide firebox, as a direct development of the 'Klondikes'. Nº 251, the first of the large-boiler Atlantics, became symbolic of the GNR, and the locomotive was featured heavily in the GNR's advertising. The large-boiler Atlantics were superb performers on the East Coast express trains and were surpassed

only by the much larger and more-powerful Gresley Pacifics, such as *Flying Scotsman*.

As explained in the previous chapter, from 1896 Douglas Earle Marsh worked for the GNR as Chief Assistant Mechanical Engineer at Doncaster, where he assisted H. A. Ivatt in the design of the legendary 'Klondike' small-boiler Atlantics. When later he assumed control at Brighton he discovered that a new design of large express locomotive was urgently required and so used his earlier GNR connections to obtain from Doncaster a set of drawings for Ivatt's subsequent 'Large Atlantic' design, to which he made few amendments before

ordering five locomotives, to be constructed by Kitson & Co of Leeds. It was not surprising, therefore, that the LBSCR's first 4-4-2 tender engines, which appeared in 1905/6, bore a marked similarity to their cousins on the GNR. The largest locomotives to run on the Brighton line prior to the Grouping, they were, quite naturally, assigned to its fastest and most prestigious trains.

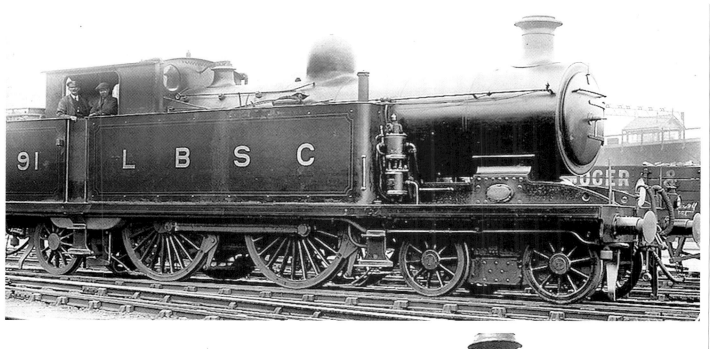

As well as the H1 class and H2 class express tender locomotive designs, which were primarily of GNR design, Douglas Earle Marsh also designed four versions of 4-4-2 tank Atlantic locomotive classes; the I1, I2, I3 & I4. These locomotives were also based on GNR design and practice. Here is Nº 91, the last member of the I3 class to be built and completed in March 1913. It was withdrawn from Brighton Depot forty years later. (Author)

D. E. Marsh's 4-4-2 tank locomotives were based on the GNR's C12 version. Nº 4546, was originally completed in August 1907 by GNR and originally numbered Nº 1546. It is seen here in LNER livery and was withdrawn in June 1947, just before Nationalisation. (Author)

The LBSCR's Atlantic design of locomotive was a very similar machine to its cousin on the GNR and both types worked the quickest and most prestigious services. H. A. Ivatt's large boiler design Atlantic locomotive N° 279 is seen working the prestigious '*Flying Scotsman*' service through Hadley Wood as seen here in a contemporary illustration. (Author)

Seen on the front of an advertising brochure is N° 41, the last member of the batch of five of D. E. Marsh's Atlantic design locomotive. The H1 class of locomotive is seen working the prestigious '*Southern Belle*' Pullman service to Brighton. (Author)

Chapter 6

BRIGHTON WORKS

Brighton Works was one of the earliest railway-owned repair facilities constructed anywhere in the world, even pre-dating the more famous railway works at Crewe, Doncaster and Swindon. Established in 1840, by the London & Brighton Railway, the works grew steadily between 1841 and 1900, but the efficient operation of the works was always hampered by its location on a very restricted site, and over the years there were many plans to close it and move the facility elsewhere. Nevertheless, between 1852 and 1957, more than 1,200 steam locomotives were constructed there.

Notable steam locomotives constructed at Brighton over the years included the Stroudley-designed Class A1 'Terrier' 0-6-0Ts (one of which, Nº 40 *Brighton*, was awarded a Gold Medal at the 1878 Exposition Universelle in Paris), Stroudley's last express passenger locomotives, his Class B1 'Gladstone' 0-4-2s (of which Nº 189 *Edward Blount* was awarded a Gold Medal at the 1889 Exposition Universelle), R. J. Billinton's B4 4-4-0s and D3 0-4-4Ts, Marsh's H2 Atlantics and 4-4-2 tank engines of Classes I1, I2, I3 and I4 and L. B. Billinton's L class 4-6-4 tanks. The last steam locomotive to be built

at Brighton was a British Railways Standard Class 4MT 2-6-4 tank, Nº 80154, which was out-shopped on 20 March 1957. Prototype steam, electric and diesel-electric locomotives were also constructed there, before the eventual closure of the facility in 1962. After its use as a factory for constructing 'bubble cars', it was demolished and the site has since been redeveloped as part of the 'New Brighton Quarter'.

During the early years at Brighton locomotives were bought in from specialist builders of variable repute; these included Sharp, Roberts & Co, Jones, Turner & Evans, Fairbairn, Forrester, Rennies and Hawthorns. In the rapidly developing era of new

technology, many different problems were encountered, which sometimes caused the late delivery of locomotives and occasionally, after the locomotives had been delivered, they often suffered from poor reliability. This situation was not acceptable by the LBSCR's directors. So they decided to set up a proper locomotive works at Brighton, with a chief engineer in charge to take responsibility for the situation and create an environment where reliability was to be the name of the game.

Over the years numerous engineers have held the post of Locomotive Superintendent for the Brighton line, these being:

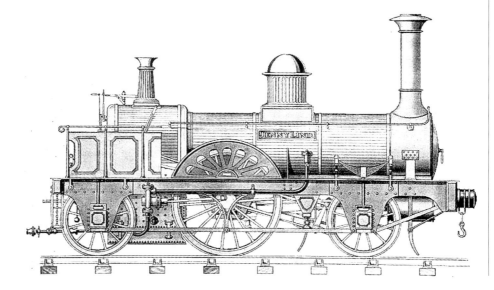

Jenny Lind was the first of a class of ten steam locomotives built in 1847 for the London, Brighton and South Coast Railway - LBSCR, by E. B. Wilson & Co of Leeds. The general design of the locomotive proved to be very successful and the manufacturers adopted it for use on other railways. It became the first "mass-produced" locomotive type to a constructed to a consistent pattern. Indeed, if the buyer wanted changes from the standard design he would be liable to pay for any modifications or changes. The Jenny type, was named after Jenny Lind, who was a famous opera singer of that period. (Author)

William Stroudley
was one of Britain's
most famous steam
locomotive engineers of
the nineteenth century,
and worked principally
for the London, Brighton
and South Coast Railway.
He designed some
of the most famous,
elegant and long-lived
steam locomotives of
his era. In 1870, he was
appointed Locomotive
Superintendent of the
LBSCR at Brighton
Works and is seen here
standing alongside one
of his masterpieces; the
diminutive LBSCR A1
class 0-6-0 "Terrier"
tank locomotive N° 40,
Brighton. Indeed, N° 40
Brighton, which entered
service on 10 March
1878, was awarded
a Gold Medal at the
Exposition Universelle,
Paris in 1878. N° 40
Brighton has been
preserved and can be
seen on the Isle of Wight
Railway. (Author)

W. C. Harrison (1838-42)
Thomas Statham (1840-3)
John Gray (1845-7)
Thomas Kirtley (1847)
John Chester Craven (1847-70)
William Stroudley (1870-89)
Robert John Billinton (1890-1904)
Douglas Earle Marsh (1904-11)
Lawson Boskovsky Billinton
(1912-22)

The London & Brighton Railway
was incorporated in 1837 and
survived until 1846. Its first
Locomotive Superintendent is
recorded as being one W. C.
Harrison, who took up the position
in 1838 and had the daunting task
of setting up a complete operating
railway system from naught.

In 1840 the London & Brighton
Railway opened its railway
works at Brighton, this being one
of the earliest railway-operated
locomotive workshops. In the same
year Thomas Statham joined W.
C. Harrison to carry out the duties
of Locomotive Superintendent for
the London & Brighton Railway.
Harrison departed in 1842, leaving
Statham to continue on his own
until the end of 1843.

Although the principal works
for servicing locomotives had
yet to be established at Brighton,
a small facility for 'day to day'
repair work was badly needed
and was opened in May 1840. It
consisted of a small locomotive
shed constructed northwest of the
station, on the London & Brighton
Railway's Brighton–Shoreham
line. The following year, when
the London–Brighton main line
opened throughout, a larger repair
facility and motive-power depot
was opened adjacent to Brighton
Station, situated in the 'V' formed

by the present West Coastway Line
and the main line to London. It
was fully equipped with an eight-
road shed, turntable, wheel-drop
and weigh-bridge. In 1959 the
shed was home to 60 locomotives,
but it closed in 1964, the site now
being occupied by the Combined
Engineering Depot.

John Gray was an early steam-
locomotive engineer, but his precise
origins are unknown. He appears
to have come from Newcastle and
introduced several innovations in
steam-locomotive design during
the 1830s and '40s. In 1838, working
for the Liverpool & Manchester
Railway, he became the first
engineer to use the 'balanced
slide valve' on locomotives. This
is where the system gave some of
the advantages of a piston valve,
to a slide valve, by relieving the
pressure on the back of the valve
and so helping to reduce friction
and wear. In 1840 he was appointed
Locomotive Superintendent of
the Hull & Selby Railway, where
he became the first engineer to
use long-travel valve motion.
In 1845 he took up a similar
position on the Croydon, Dover &
Brighton Joint Committee, which
at that time operated the pooled
locomotive fleets of the London
& Croydon Railway, the South
Eastern Railway and the London
& Brighton Railway; upon the
dissolution of this committee and
the formation of the LBSCR in 1846
Gray was appointed Locomotive
Superintendent at Brighton
Railway Works, but in 1847 he was
dismissed from his post, as a result
of problems with the late delivery
of locomotives from Timothy
Hackworth.

The son of a colliery owner
and the elder brother of Matthew,
Thomas Kirtley was born at
Tanfield, County Durham, and
began his career as a driver on
the Liverpool & Manchester
Railway. In 1837 he founded
Warrington-based locomotive
builder Thomas Kirtley & Co, but
the company failed in 1841. After
briefly working for his brother
on the Warrington & Newton
Railway he was in 1843 appointed
Locomotive Superintendent of the
North Midland Railway, but he
lost this role upon the formation of
the Midland Railway in May 1844,
thereafter serving as an inspector. In
1845 he was working on the Trent
Valley line for Thomas Brassey, and
in February 1847 he was appointed
Locomotive Superintendent of the
LBSCR following the dismissal of
John Gray. Nine months later he
suffered a brain tumour and died.

Born near Leeds on 11 September
1813, John Chester Craven worked
on the Manchester and Leeds
Railway and then the Eastern
Counties Railway, before joining
the LBSCR in 1847 as Locomotive,
Carriage & Wagon Superintendent.
He expanded and improved the
locomotive facilities at Brighton,
making it possible for locomotives
to be constructed there, rather than
being 'bought in' from outside
contractors. But he became famous
for creating an excessively large
number of locomotive classes,
believing in matching each
particular locomotive to a specific
line or route job. By the end of the
1860s this policy was no longer
acceptable and he was approached
by the Board of Directors about this
situation, whereupon he resigned

Completed in November 1887, LB&SCR 2-2-2- N° 490 *Dieppe* was scrapped in April 1896; the approximate date of this image. Built by Robert Stephenson & Co., its original number was N° 200. (John Scott-Morgan)

in November 1869. John Craven had also been responsible for changing the proposed plan for the relocation of the works to Horley, keeping them at Brighton instead. An acknowledged authority on docks and canal locks, he continued to advise on these matters into his retirement and died on 27 June 1887.

In the early days the LBSCR's passenger carriages were built by contractors at New Cross Gate, just down the line from London Bridge, but in 1848, under the direction of Craven, construction was moved to Brighton. Craven also set about enlarging and equipping Brighton Works for locomotive construction, although its location, close to the main line, in an area which would soon become built up, always imposed restrictions that mitigate against efficient operation. The first locomotive to be built at Brighton

was LBSCR N° 14, a 2-2-2, in May 1852.

During 1860 Craven began the removal from the west side of the main line of a large mound of chalk that had been dumped there during the line's construction. The space created was used to accommodate a new and much enlarged motive-power depot in 1861, permitting the closure of the existing facilities and incorporating them into the works proper, but by 1866 consideration was again being given to concentrating repairs at the railway works located adjacent to New Cross Gate station.

There is no doubt that Craven built useful and reliable locomotives, but he did not believe in standardising locomotive designs, instead producing classes of one or two locomotives designed for specific tasks. This was expensive, as components had to be produced individually rather

than in batches, which would have helped to reduce manufacturing costs. Eventually this resulted in a chaotic maintenance situation, which proved his downfall. By 1869 there were no fewer 72 different designs of locomotive in use, and, when pressed by the LBSCR's directors to reduce this number, Craven offered his resignation. This was accepted, and 1870 he was superseded as Locomotive Superintendent by William Stroudley.

Born on 6 March 1833 at Sandford-on-Thames in Oxfordshire, William Stroudley was one of Britain's most famous steam locomotive engineers of the nineteenth century. Beginning work in 1847 at his local paper mill, in the same year he was apprenticed to John Inshaw, a mechanic and inventor who owned an engineering company in Birmingham, and over the next seven years he

Craven-built 2-2-2
N° 196 *Pevensey* was completed in December 1865 as a replacement to earlier built engines on the Brighton Line. It ended its days in October 1890. (John Scott-Morgan)

The LB&SCR Belgravia class 2-4-0 passenger locomotives were designed by William Stroudley in 1872 for secondary passenger duties. When Stroudley took up his duties as Locomotive Superintendent at the Brighton works of the LB&SCR in 1870, he found that some locomotive components which had been ordered by his predecessor, John Chester Craven, had not been used. The LB&SCR Belgravia class 2-4-0 passenger locomotives were designed by William Stroudley in 1872 for secondary passenger duties. When Stroudly took up his duties as Locomotive Superintendent at the Brighton works of the LB&SCR in 1870, he found that some locomotives components which had been ordered by his predecessor, John Chester Craven, had not been used and so Stroudley produced a new design of 2-4-0 to use these fraomes. Engine No 202 was one of these engines and was named Goodwood. It was completed in 1872. (John Scott-Morgan)

gained engineering experience on stationary engines and steam barges.

From 1854 Stroudley trained as a locomotive engineer at the Great Western Railway's Swindon Works, under Daniel Gooch. He then moved to the Great Northern Railway, working under Charles Sacré at its Peterborough workshops, where he later became the running foreman at the locomotive depot. In 1861 he was appointed Manager of the Edinburgh & Glasgow Railway's Cowlairs Works. Staying in Scotland, he moved on in June 1865, to become appointed as the Locomotive & Carriage Superintendent of the Highland Railway at Inverness, but he was frustrated there, as the railway had no money, and he was able to produce just one locomotive. He was, however, able to reorganise and modernise the company's Lochgorm Works and to reduce the operating costs for the railway's existing fleet.

Stroudley moved on again, and in 1870 he was appointed Locomotive Superintendent of the LBSCR, following Craven's enforced resignation. When he took up his office, he discovered that were 72 different classes of locomotive in use and that there was an urgent need for standardisation to reduce operating costs. Again Stroudley was hampered by the difficult financial state of his new company, which had faced bankruptcy in

This was the last design from John Chester Craven, the LBSCR's locomotive superintendent. The class of six served the line for about 30 years. Five were scrapped from 1894-1896, with the sixth example retained as a 'pumper'. Seen here is Nº 468, which was constructed by Avonside in 1868 and had 5ft driving wheels with Stephenson valve gear. The tender had a water capacity of 2,400 gallons. (John Scott-Morgan)

1866. But during the 1870s and '80s increased revenues, particularly from the growth of suburban traffic, enabled Stroudley to dramatically improve the performance and reliability of the locomotive stock by introducing a number of very successful classes.

Stroudley's first passenger-locomotive design for the LBSCR, in 1872, was the 'Belgravia' 2-4-0, which was remarkably similar to the 2-4-0s constructed at Cowlairs Works for the Edinburgh & Glasgow Railway while he was Works Manager there in the early 1860s. Upon taking up his duties at Brighton Works in 1870 he had discovered that some locomotive

components had been ordered by his predecessor, Craven, and these included six sets of frames for some 2-4-0 passenger locomotives designed by Craven. Stroudley decided to put these frames to good use and produced a new design of 2-4-0 in order to use them, so the six locomotives of the 'Belgravia' class incorporated many features of his later designs. Also in 1872 he introduced the first of three important tank-engine designs that were ultimately produced in large numbers, this being the diminutive Class A1 ('Terrier') 0-6-0T. A number of these locomotives remained in use in the 1960s,

and thankfully several have been preserved.

Stroudley's D1 0-4-2 tank engines were used for the London suburban services from 1873 until electrification, and some survived until the late 1940s. A larger version of his D2 design (itself developed from his successful D1 tank engine of 1873), the 'Richmond' 0-4-2 express passenger locomotive, designed by Stroudley in 1877, was truly magnificent. Built at Brighton and placed in traffic between October 1878 and March 1880, the six examples of this class replaced earlier Craven locomotives on the heaviest express trains between London and Brighton. Performing

As previously mentioned, the necessity to 'use-up' components produced by Craven meant that the 2-4-0 locomotives had a number of design features, such as double frames, which were not found with Stroudley's later designs and were the heaviest 2-4-0 locomotives of their time. At first the class suffered from poor steaming, but once this was rectified they went on to give reliable service on secondary passenger trains, as well as working the "business" expresses between London Bridge and Brighton until about 1881. Under Stroudley's locomotive classification scheme, the *Belgravia* class, being main line express engines, were included in the B class. By the time that the B class was subdivided into B1, B2, etc. by D. E. Marsh, none of the *Belgravia* class remained in service. Here is the first locomotive of the class called *Belgravia*, after which the class was named. (Author)

well on these duties for a decade, they were eventually replaced by Stroudley's larger B1s, the first of which, N° 214 *Gladstone*, is preserved at the National Railway Museum at York.

During his time with the LBSCR Stroudley reorganised and modernised Brighton Works along with the repair facilities at New Cross, and he is also remembered for inventing the re-railing ramps that are still known as Stroudley's Patent Ramps.

Like his predecessors, Stroudley considered moving the main repair works at Brighton to the site at Horley, but instead he chose to move the carriage-repair shed and paint shops to new sites on the western side of the main line at Brighton, transferring the marine-engineering work undertaken by the works to a new facility at Newhaven. When this reorganisation was completed, this

allowed for further enlargement of the locomotive repair and construction facilities, which included the addition of an iron foundry in 1873 and a new carriage painting and cleaning shop in 1878 and a coppersmith's shop in 1881. This solved many problem for a while, but did not address the underlying issue of the inadequate site. By the end of the century, the Works was again suffering from difficulties affecting its efficient operation.

William Love, senior driver on the LBSCR, once told a story that while he was standing by his locomotive and waiting to be signalled on to his train, Stroudley come along and asked him: 'How is it, Love, that you always run through Haywards Heath without taking water?' Love replied that he '…always started off with a full cold tender of water'. Stroudley paused for a moment before striking his

umbrella on the footplate and exclaiming: 'Of course! I didn't think of that. You do not expand your water by heating it!' It had been customary for drivers at this time to pre-heat their water by 'knocking' the steam back into the tender and so they did not start off with as much water. The reasons being that some of the water in the tender was expanded by heating it with boiler steam and that some of the water was wasted, as steam was passed back into the tender during this preheating process, the net result being that there was not as much water available in the tender, than if the water had been cold throughout. Love was chosen to accompany 'Gladstone' 0-4-2 N° 189 *Edward Blount* to the 1889 Exposition Universelle in Paris, where it won a Gold Medal. Stroudley died whilst attending the exhibition, having caught an infection there.

Born in Wakefield *c*1845, Robert John Billinton was the son of a railway contractor and in 1859 was apprenticed to William Fairbairn & Sons, of Manchester. By 1860 J. Simpson & Co, specialists in the manufacturing of pumps, had moved to a new factory by the River Thames at 101 Grosvenor Road, Pimlico, and in 1863 Billinton moved there. In 1866 the company built a steam locomotive for the Southampton Dock Co and the same year constructed two rotative beam engines for Tunbridge Wells Waterworks. Soon afterwards Billinton moved to the Calderdale Iron Works, where he worked with Roland Child, mining and civil engineers of Wakefield. He then became assistant works manager to Munro, Walker and

William Stroudley was the Chief Mechanical Engineer of the LBSCR from 1869-1889. On 31 December 1882, the first of Stroudley's final design of express passenger locomotives, Nº 214 *Gladstone*, left Brighton Works. A total of thirty-six B1 class locomotives were turned out between 1882 and 1889. The *Gladstones*, which were used for the heaviest London to Brighton express trains, were named after politicians, men associated with the railway and places served by the railway. Nº 214 *Gladstone* was bought by the Stephenson Locomotive Society in 1927 and is now part of the collection of the NRM. Nº 214 *Gladstone* is seen here at Battersea Shed before preservation. (John Scott-Morgan)

The LBSCR's B4 class engines worked the heaviest express trains until around 1912, when they were gradually replaced by the larger classes, and were then used on slower and lighter services. Most of R. J. Billington's B4 class engines, were made by Sharpe, Stewart & Co, hence their nickname "Scotchmen". N° 53 was built at Brighton in 1900 and had a "Hotchkiss" water circulator fitted from 1906 until 1915. N° 53 *Richmond* is seen waiting to depart with the 17:58 London Bridge to Portsmouth service. O. S. Nock said that the B4 class engines '… were among the finest passenger locomotives of their day'. N° 53 finally went for scrap in 1935.
(Ernie Pay)

Easton of Sheffield, where he was responsible for the design and building of railway locomotives and stationary engines. In 1870 Billinton was appointed assistant to William Stroudley at Brighton Works. In 1874 he moved to become assistant to Samuel W. Johnson on the Midland Railway at Derby, but following Stroudley's death in December 1889 Billinton returned to Brighton and was appointed as Stroudley's successor the following month.

During his time at Brighton Billinton was responsible for a number of successful locomotive designs, including the D Class (later D3) 0-4-4T, the C2 0-6-0 and the B4 4-4-0. He also designed four types of radial tank engine, Classes E3, E4, E5 and E6. Many of his locomotives were rebuilt with larger boilers by his successor, D. E. Marsh. Billinton also introduced new classes of steel-framed carriage stock and reorganised and enlarged the locomotive and carriage facilities at Brighton. He died in office on 7 November 1904.

Douglas Earle Marsh succeeded R. J. Billinton as Locomotive, Carriage & Wagon Superintendent at Brighton Works on 23 November 1904, his locomotives including two classes of Atlantic tender engine (H1 and H2) and four types of Atlantic tank engine (Classes I1, I2, I3 and I4). In 1910 he designed a 4-6-2 tank engine (of which just two examples were built: one J1 and one J2), but his least-successful design was the C3 goods 0-6-0 of 1906. Whilst at Brighton he abolished the yellow livery for passenger locomotives and decreed that their names be removed.

From 1905 Brighton Works found itself unable to keep pace with the number of locomotives requiring servicing, and a backlog

began to build up. As a result the LBSCR established concentrations of locomotives awaiting their turn to enter works, at such locations as East Grinstead, Horsted Keynes and Horley. In 1908 Robert Urie, then Works Manager at Nine Elms, on the London & South Western Railway, was asked to conduct an outside investigation into the causes of this build-up of unserviceable locomotives. He discovered that 108 of the LBSCR's 541 locomotives — 20 per cent of the stock — were undergoing repair or awaiting attention. It was also found out that, a general overhaul at Brighton Works took on average 43 days to complete, compared with 21 days taken by the South Eastern & Chatham Railway at its works at Ashford. By 1910 some 30 per cent of the locomotive fleet was unserviceable due to the delays and inefficiencies at Brighton Works.

Born on 4 February 1882, the son of R. J. Billinton, Lawson Butzkopfski (sometimes shown as Boskovsky) Billinton served the LBSCR as Locomotive, Carriage & Wagon Superintendent from 1912 until the end of its existence in 1922. He had joined the company in 1900 as an apprentice, and by the end of 1907 he was Locomotive Superintendent at New Cross Gate. He sought to lighten the backlog of locomotives waiting repair by executing repairs and boiler

A view of a pre-grouping *'Southern Belle'* service, with LBSCR Atlantic N° 41 heading a Pullman car express, along the Brighton main line. (John Scott-Morgan)

This view of Brighton Works shows various locomotives in different stages of repair. On the right is Stroudley Terrier A1 class 0-6-0T locomotive N° 56 *Shoreditch*, which entered service on 18 November 1875. It was finally sold for £125 to George Cohen & Co. in August 1903 and was scrapped at Redhill. (John Scott-Morgan)

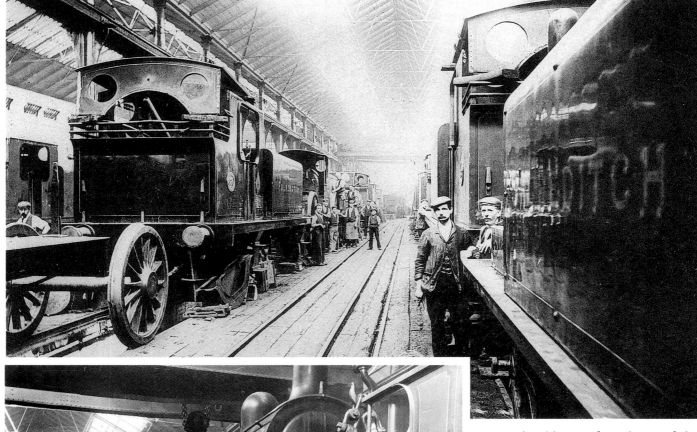

Another view of Brighton Works during the LB&SCR era. Here the LB&SCR's B4 class 4-4-0 N° 54 *Empress* is seen being lifted at Brighton Works N° 2 erecting shop. (John Scott-Morgan)

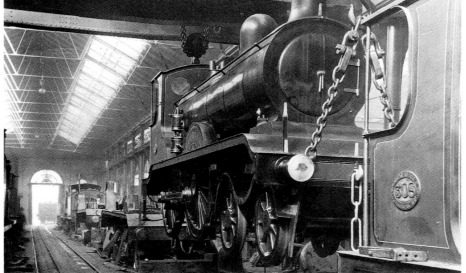

changes, but this had little effect. Marsh took much of the blame for the problem and was granted leave of absence due to sickness in 1910, resigning in July 1911.

Billinton had been invited to take over on a temporary basis during Marsh's sickness and promptly set about reorganising the works and reducing the backlog by using

emerging 'time and motion study' techniques. The basic problem at Brighton was that the works was overwhelmed with work. In 1910 land was bought at Lancing for a new carriage and wagon works, which was opened in 1912. This allowed Stroudley's carriage shed to be used as an overflow 'stock shed' by the locomotive works and the motive power depot. Engines repaired at Brighton were also sometimes taken to Lancing for final painting. In 1913 Billinton put before the LBSCR board proposals to close Brighton Works and to concentrate all locomotive construction and repair work at a new facility adjacent to the carriage works at Lancing, but the outbreak

of the First World War in 1914 put paid to this plan. During his time at Brighton he designed the E2 Class 0-6-0 tank engines and K Class 2-6-0s (both introduced in 1913) and the L Class 4-6-4 tanks (1914).

Locomotive construction at Brighton ceased with the completion of the last E2 0-6-0T and K Class 2-6-0s at the end of 1916, halfway through the war, the works then becoming involved in munitions production. After the war there was again a substantial backlog of repairs and new construction did not resume

until late 1920. The last locomotive to be built at the works by the LBSCR was L Class 4-6-4T N° 333 *Remembrance*, completed in April 1922.

Formed at the Grouping in 1923, the Southern Railway inherited locomotive works at Brighton, Eastleigh and Ashford, new construction thereafter being concentrated at the latter two facilities. For the entirety of its existence the Southern had just two Chief Mechanical Engineers, these being R. E. L. Maunsell (1923-37) and O. V. S. Bulleid (1937-47).

Richard Edward Lloyd Maunsell was born on 26 May 1868 at Raheny, County Dublin, in Ireland. He began an apprenticeship at the Inchicore works of the Great Southern & Western Railway under Henry Alfred Ivatt (of later GNR fame) in 1886, completing his training at Horwich Works on the Lancashire & Yorkshire Railway, much as Nigel Gresley had done before. After Horwich he worked as locomotive foreman in charge of the Blackpool and Fleetwood District. From there, in 1894, he went to India, as the Assistant Locomotive

The Brighton Baltic tanks were the last LBSCR Locomotives constructed at Brighton Works. Seven examples were built between April 1914 and April 1922 and they were used for express passenger services. They were kept fully occupied on the main express services between London and Brighton until the line was electrified in 1933. This image shows number 332 on a Pullman car express, c.1922. (John Scott-Morgan)

Having 6ft driving wheels, the prototype K class engine N° 790 *River Avon* was built under SECR ownership and was one of twenty members of the ill-fated 2-6-4T "River" class. Following the derailment of K class engine N° A800 *River Cray* at Sevenoaks, a rebuilding program was begun at Ashford Works in June 1928 and involved converting a 2-6-4 tank engine into a 2-6-0 tender engine. Included was the removal of the side water tanks, rear coal bunker and trailing axles, but the 6ft driving wheels, right-hand drive and N class type boiler were retained. Here we see 795 River Medway with a passenger service on the Quarry Line, c.1927. (John Scott-Morgan)

Superintendent of the East Indian Railway Co, subsequently becoming District Locomotive Superintendent of the Asansol District. He returned in 1896 to become Works Manager at the Inchicore, Dublin, works of the GSWR, being promoted to Locomotive Superintendent in 1911. Then, in 1913, he was selected to succeed Harry Wainwright as CME of the South Eastern & Chatham Railway. When that line was incorporated in the new Southern Railway he became the latter's Chief

Mechanical Engineer, eventually retiring in 1937.

For the first three years of the Southern Railway's existence no new locomotives were built at Brighton, although the B4s were rebuilt as virtually new locomotives in the period 1922-4. During 1926 the works was responsible for building 10 examples of Maunsell's 'River' Class 2-6-4Ts, and the subsequent rebuilding of six of them as U Class 2-6-0 tender engines took place two years later.

Brighton Atlantic Nº 2421 is seen receiving attention at Brighton Works during its Southern Railway days. As can be seen from its nameplates, it was named *South Foreland*. (John Scott-Morgan)

The works also built a further 10 new U Class Moguls in 1928. The following year the Brighton Works constructed all of Maunsell's Z Class 0-8-0 tank engines, before locomotive construction ceased once again.

By 1931, with the impending electrification of the main line, Brighton Works once again seemed likely to close. Many of the skilled workmen and much of the equipment were transferred to Eastleigh and Ashford. The paint shop was converted into a maintenance facility for electric multiple-units, and the former carriage shed was adapted for use by the SR's new Engineers' Department, while the locomotive depot was rebuilt and reduced in size.

Oliver Vaughan Snell Bulleid was born in Invercargill, New Zealand, but on the death of his father in 1889 he moved with his mother to Llanfyllin, Wales, where his family home had originally been. After a technical education at Accrington he joined the Great Northern Railway at Doncaster as an apprentice to H. A. Ivatt. After a four-year apprenticeship he became the Assistant to the Locomotive Running Superintendent, and a year later he was appointed Works Manager at Doncaster. In 1908 he left to work in Paris as a test engineer with the French division of Westinghouse Electric Corporation, being soon promoted to Assistant Works Manager and Chief Draughtsman, and later that year he married Marjorie Ivatt, the youngest daughter of Henry Ivatt. There followed a brief period working for the Board of Trade (from 1910), where he arranged exhibitions in Brussels, Paris and Turin. During this time he was able to travel widely in Europe, including a trip with Gresley, Stanier and Hawksworth to Belgium to see a metre-gauge bogie locomotive. In December 1912 he rejoined the GNR as assistant to Nigel Gresley, its recently appointed CME. During

The decision to electrify the entire main line from London to Brighton was taken in 1929, with the section from Coulsdon North to Three Bridges being opened in July 1932. The section from Three Bridges to Brighton was operational from 1 January 1933. The Southern Railway gave the designations 6PUL, 6CITY and 6PAN to electric multiple units built to work the routes from London to Brighton and West Worthing to Eastbourne. Here are two 6PUL electric units which both had a Pullman Car included in the trains formation. (John Scott-Morgan)

The last of the trio of the Bulleid/Raworth designed electric locomotives, N° 20003 was constructed in 1948 at Brighton Works. It is seen here in a contemporary view working a passenger service out of Victoria on Grosvenor Bank. This engine along with the two others in its class was partially responsible for eliminating the Atlantics from the Victoria - Newhaven Boat Train services. (Author)

the First World War Bulleid joined the British Army and was assigned to the rail-transport arm, rising to the rank of Major, and following the end of hostilities he returned to the GNR as Manager of the Wagon & Carriage Works. At the Grouping in 1923 Nigel Gresley was appointed Chief Mechanical Engineer of the London & North Eastern Railway, bringing Bulleid back to Doncaster to be his assistant, and it was in the following years that he produced the majority of his famous designs, Bulleid lending a hand with many, including the P1 and P2 2-8-2s, the U1 2-8-0+0-8-2 Garratt and, arguably his masterpiece, the A4 Pacific.

In 1937, following Maunsell's retirement, Bulleid accepted the post of CME of the Southern Railway. In 1938 he gained approval to build the 'Merchant Navy' Pacifics, drawing on his experiences from across Europe and using the most modern equipment available with a partially welded boiler and firebox rather than traditional riveted designs.

Bulleid played a major role in the electrification of the SR, including infrastructure, electric multiple-units and electric locomotives. He was also responsible for the design and construction of Britain's only double-deck passenger trains,

the two '4-DD' units. Bulleid also had responsibility for coaching stock, an area in which he had an active interest. His designs were built on the best of the existing designs, while making his own improvements. His passenger coaches were known for their comfort and spaciousness and were indeed popular with the travelling public. Many of the design features — such as the size and layout details, were used by British Railways for its standard Mk 1 passenger coaches.

Bulleid's final design of steam locomotive for the Southern Railway was the unconventional 'Leader' 0-6-6-0T, the first example of which did not emerge until after nationalisation in 1949. The boiler, coal and water supplies were all enclosed in a smooth double-ended body, which to modern eyes is reminiscent of that of a diesel or electric locomotive. Drive was via two six-wheel powered bogies, each having three cylinders, each one powering a single axle, by chain drive. Although the 'Leader' was highly innovative for its time it was deemed unsuccessful. The driver had a very pleasant improved environment, but the poor fireman, trapped by his firebox door, with little hope of escape, was in danger of being roasted alive. If the locomotive had been oil-fired it might have had a feature, but after Bulleid had left British Railways and moved to Ireland the project was cancelled.

Fears of air-raid attacks on Ashford and Eastleigh, along with the need for more steam locomotives and munitions during the Second World War,

H1 class Atlantic Nº 2039 by now named *Hartland Point* during late Southern Railway/early British Railways days whilst she was being used as a test bed for Bulleid's sleeve valve design for his Leader project. Nº 2039 is also fitted with an experimental large diameter chimney and multiple jet blast pipe. (John Scott-Morgan)

The Leader class of experimental steam locomotive was produced to the design of the innovative engineer O. V. S. Bulleid, in an attempt to extend the life of steam traction by eliminating many of the operational drawbacks associated with existing steam locomotives. Problems with the design and indifferent reports on performance and political pressure surrounding spiralling development costs, led to all locomotives of the class being scrapped by 1951. Here Nº 36001 is seen after one of its test workings. (Author)

O. V. S. Bulleid's light Pacifics were designed to work over the restricted secondary routes of the Southern Railway. Nº 21C164 *Fighter Command* was the thousandth locomotive to be built at Brighton Works. Numbered as 34064 Fighter Command it was sent to Nine Elms Depot, as seen here to be prepared as the Stand-by for Sir Winston Churchill's funeral train, but was not used. Nº 34064 was fitted with a Giesel Oblong Ejector & Spark Arrester. The ejector's efficiency overcame the resistance caused by the mesh of the spark arrester, without spoiling the steaming. BR paid a license fee for its use and this was a major factor not to fit any more. However, Nº 34064 was withdrawn at Basingstoke in 1966, after a 'high speed wheel slip' between Farnborough and Basingstoke, which resulted in bending its coupling rods. Nº 34064 is seen here at Nine Elms shed prior to being despatched to Staines. (Ernie Pay)

brought about the reopening and re-equipping of the workshops at Brighton in 1941. Then, throughout the remaining years of the war, Brighton Works was used for the construction of steam locomotives, initially for the Southern Railway but also later on for the War Department, the London, Midland & Scottish Railway and the London & North Eastern Railway, but it also manufactured component parts for tanks and anti-aircraft guns. The workshops were damaged during the Brighton Blitz of May 1943, but the damage was soon repaired.

During the Second World War Brighton Works built more than half of Bulleid's Q1 0-6-0 freight locomotives, and the Brighton drawing office was primarily responsible for the detailed designs of his revolutionary 'Merchant Navy' Pacifics, although these were built at Eastleigh. From 1943 Brighton built 93 of the LMS-designed 8F 2-8-0 freight locomotives for use by the War Department, at the astonishing rate of one every 4½ days.

The heyday of steam-locomotive construction at Brighton was arguably the decade immediately following the Second World War, when the works built more than 100 of O. V. S. Bulleid's Light Pacifics. It also constructed the boilers and tenders for the final batch of 10 'Merchant Navy' Pacifics, although these, like the earlier examples, were erected at Eastleigh.

Bulleid's Light Pacifics were designed to work over the restricted secondary routes of the Southern Railway. Two naming themes were used, creating the 'West Country' and 'Battle of Britain' classes, the

The first two members of British Railways' D16/2 class of diesel-electric locomotives were built at Ashford Works and were introduced in 1950–1951. The third member, Nº 10203, was out-shopped from Brighton Works in March 1954. Its modified engine gave a power output of 2,000 hp. Tested on the Southern Region it then joined its sisters on the London Midland and was allocated to Willesden depot. All three locomotives were non-standard with regards to spare parts and servicing and so were withdrawn at the end of 1963. After spending some time on the scrap line at Derby Works they were eventually scrapped by Cashmore's at their Great Bridge scrapyard in 1968. This is a front end look at Nº 10203 soon after completion. (Author)

latter honouring personalities, aircraft types, RAF stations and RAF squadrons involved in or connected with the famous airborne conflict of 1940. Nº 21C164 *Fighter Command* was the 1,000th steam locomotive to be built at Brighton Works and was completed in June 1947.

In 1948 the Southern Railway was nationalised, becoming the Southern Region of British Railways, and

With the design work done at Brighton for the whole class and with the overall programme being overseen by Robert Riddles, the last steam locomotive to be built at Brighton Works was British Railways Standard Class 4MT 2-6-4 tank locomotive Nº 80154. It entered service on Sunday, 26 March 1957 and was allocated to Brighton, with the shed code 75A. (Ernie Pay)

under the new regime Brighton Works was once again used for new-locomotive construction, Brighton staff being responsible for the design and/or construction of three of the most successful BR Standard classes — the Class 4 4-6-0s and 2-6-4Ts and the Class 9F 2-10-0 heavy-freight locomotives. From 1951 Brighton built 130 Class 4 tank engines, new construction finally ceasing in 1957 with the completion of Nº 80154, the 1,211th locomotive to be built at Brighton.

Besides the 0-6-6-0T 'Leaders', prototype locomotives constructed at Brighton included the third in the series of the Bulleid-designed Co-Co electrics, Nº 20003, in 1948 and the third of the Bulleid 1Co-Co1 diesel-electrics, Nº 10203, in 1954. The bogie design and the power train of Nº 10203 were used almost unmodified for the first 10 English Electric Type 4 (Class 40) diesel-electrics in 1958. The works also produced turntables

and other heavy items of railway infrastructure.

At the time of the centenary of steam-locomotive construction at Brighton, in 1952, the works covered nine acres and employed about 650 staff. But in the Modernisation Plan for BR, announced in 1955, Brighton Works was once again passed over. Locomotive repairs ceased in 1958, although the buildings would survive until 1969. The motive-power depot was officially closed on 15 June 1961, but the building remained in use for stabling steam locomotives until 1964, finally being demolished in 1966.

Following the closure of the main works at Brighton part of the building was used between 1957 and 1964 for assembly of the Isetta, an Italian-designed 'micro-car' built under licence. Because of its egg shape and bubble-like windows, it became known as a 'bubble car'.

With regard to the rest of the former works, some of the land remained in railway use, associated with the stabling of electric multiple-unit trains and other maintenance functions. Much of the site, however, became a large open car park and was used for a popular market every Sunday morning. Other land on the eastern side was given over to an assortment of retail units, including a number of car dealers with temporary structures, and a strip below the yard was used for retail premises. The final traces of Brighton Works vanished in the mid-1980s with the demolition of the elevated 1930s Southern Railway signal-box, which had supported part of the wall of the main erecting shop.

This magnificent colourful display at the Brighton Toy and Model Museum, Brighton, graphically shows a varied collection of models of various railway locomotives and rolling stock, that have over the years been associated with the Brighton Line and principally Brighton Works in particular. This is only part of a magnificent collection at the museum, which is located on the road which passes under the main Brighton Terminal Station entrance. (Author) (Courtesy of The Brighton Toy & Model Museum, Brighton)

This plaque marks the site where ISETTA OF GREAT BRITAIN LTD had its factory in the former Locomotive Engineering Works from 1957 to 1964, and where over 30,000 cars were assembled in that time. Presented by the Isetta Owners Club of Great Britain on the occasion of its 25th Anniversary.

The Isetta was a small one-door car designed in Italy, but the rights were bought by BMW. Using their existing motorbike technology, they re-engineered the car so that it initially had a 247cc 4-stroke air-cooled engined, then later a 297cc engine. In March 1957, the Brighton Locomotive Works on New England Street, finished its last railway job and six weeks later, it reopened to assemble Isettas. Two hundred or so of Brighton's workers, most of whom had worked in the locomotive works on the railway vehicles, were employed to build the new cars. As the factory had no road access, all the parts had to be brought in by railway and the assembled vehicles had to be sent out by the same method. At the height of production, 300 cars were made per week. With the Isetta having been made extinct by the BMC Mini, the bubble car era came to an end, and with it the Isetta factory, which completed its last vehicle in 1964. (Matt Smiley)

Chapter 7

NEW CROSS GATE

New Cross Gate station is sited at the foot of a two-mile uphill gradient towards Croydon. Adjacent to the station platform was built a railway locomotive works, located at the appropriately named Brighton Grove. It was the ideal location to stable locomotives used to bank trains from London Bridge up the incline. The works was operational from 1838 until the late 1940s, under the control of various railway companies. From the outset it also constructed carriages, the work being carried out by contractors, but in 1848 carriage construction was transferred to Brighton. Built by the London & Croydon Railway, the works survived various changes in ownership, passing in turn to the LBSCR, the Southern Railway and British Railways. It did, however, sustain severe air-raid damage during the Second World War and finally closed completely in 1949.

The intention was that New Cross Gate should be the location of the main goods depot and locomotive-repair workshop for the London & Croydon Railway, and indeed such facilities were opened by the LCR at Brighton Grove on 28 July 1838, just in time to receive the LCR's first locomotive, *Surrey*, although it would be almost a year before the Croydon line opened for normal traffic, on 5 June 1839 — the date that the works and New Cross Gate station opened. At this time the LCR owned seven 2-2-2s and one 0-4-2. The first five 2-2-2s and the 0-4-2 were built by Sharp, Stewart & Co and were delivered between July 1838 and July 1839; the other two locomotives were built by George & John Rennie, in August 1838 and May 1839 respectively.

In July 1841 the line through New Cross (but not the station) was also used by the London & Brighton Railway, and from 1842 to 1849 New Cross Gate station was used by the South Eastern Railway. In its early days the station was known as New Cross LBSC, being renamed New Cross Gate only after the Grouping in 1923.

In 1845/6 the station was the northern terminus of the abortive atmospheric railway from West Croydon, and until quite recently a wall of stone block sleepers, believed to be from the original London & Croydon Railway, could be seen at the southern end of the station. The station also became the southern terminus of the East London Railway line (opened in 1869) from Wapping via Brunel's Thames Tunnel. The present station structure is mid-Victorian.

Even apart from the bomb damage sustained during the

Opened on the London and Croydon Railway in 1839, on the lines that partly followed the former route of the Croydon Canal, New Station was renamed as New Cross Gate in 1923 to distinguish it from the other New Cross Station which is located to its east. This view looking towards Croydon shows the station building in the centre, with the building of the railway works located just on the right. This image was first published in June 1839, when the lines and the works opened for normal traffic. (Author)

Second World War, New Cross Gate depot appears to have suffered more than its fair share of structural damage. The original building — one of the earliest roundhouses constructed in the country — burned down in 1844, and its 1845 replacement, together with a straight shed erected by the LBSCR in 1848, was blown down in a gale in October 1863. Two replacement buildings were constructed by the LBSCR in 1863 and 1869. During this period, in 1866, consideration was given to ceasing the repair work that was then being undertaken at Brighton and to concentrating all such work at New Cross Gate, but this came to nothing.

During the 1930s, when new facilities were built at Norwood Junction — as part of a reorganisation scheme, the running sheds at New Cross Gate were run down. But with the onset of war the sheds were not formally closed until 1947 and were still used for stabling locomotives until 1951. In 1957 the buildings were all demolished, with the area replaced by sidings for the storage of electric multiple-units.

The locomotive workshops established by the LCR continued to undertake minor repairs on locomotives in the London area for the LBSCR and the SR and also briefly for British Railways. The closure of New Cross Gate depot saw some of its locomotives reallocated to Norwood Junction, but most went to Bricklayers Arms, where they were greeted as relics of the past!

A working rule was introduced whereby New Cross or Brighton duties would be covered by Brighton locomotives, and South Eastern duties by South Eastern locomotives — a sensible decision that allowed workings to continue as previously, with familiar locomotives being made available to experienced crews. Drivers that were brought up to fire through the tricky tip-flap fire-hole door of Brighton locomotives found the South Eastern fully opening sliding-door pattern easy to fire through, but it was different for the South Eastern men, some of whom took time to learn to fire Brighton locomotives.

After the reallocation of locomotives following the closure of New Cross Gate depot there was a noticeable difference in the timekeeping of certain services, in particular the 3.23am London Bridge–Brighton newspaper train, which was worked by a Brighton Atlantic tender engine. It was usual for time to be lost by the South Eastern men but rarely by the former New Cross men. But the Southern wanted good timekeeping, regardless of which crews were running the train, so the duty was re-diagrammed for a 'Schools' (Class V) 4-4-0, this being a type being familiar to the South Eastern men. Having arrived at Brighton, the 'Schools' would work a trip to Salisbury and back before returning to London later the same day with the 11pm Brighton–London Bridge mail, the locomotive finally arriving back at Bricklayers Arms depot at around 1am, before leaving again at 2.45 to work the 3.23 down — and so it went on!

The actual New Cross Gate - after which the station was named, was originally located at the junction of New Cross Road, which is behind and to the right in the picture and Queens Road, which is straight ahead in the view. This was an ideal location for a turnpike gate and booth, as it cashed in on traffic travelling on the Dover and Folkestone roads to the east and the Old Kent Road, for journeys to the City and Queens Road to the West End. The turnpike was abolished around 1865, although the horse dealer was still in business over 60 years later. (Author Collection)

Chapter 8

THE BRIGHTON PULLMANS

Pullman services were for many years an important part of the scene on the Brighton line, these prestigious passenger trains being worked originally by Craven-built locomotives of 1860 vintage. In those days the fastest journey time between London and Brighton was 65 minutes, but this was making a supreme effort, and most expresses took between 70 and 80 minutes — hardly a surprise when one considers the weight of the trains, which on occasion could comprise up to 22 coaches. Indeed, whereas the London & North Western Railway's fish train from Carlisle to London covered the 53 miles between Tebay and Preston at an average speed of 47.4mph the fastest Brighton express completed the 50.2 miles journey from London at an average of 46.6mph, prompting one wag to suggest that '…it was better to be a mackerel on the North Western than a kipper on a Pullman train on the Brighton line!'

Pullman cars had their origins in the USA, where George Mortimer Pullman pioneered the concept of providing luxury restaurant and sleeping car facilities. To travel on these services, passengers paid a premium supplement for the privilege — together with the cost of their normal train ticket.

Individual Pullman cars were introduced to Britain by the Midland Railway in 1874, being shipped from the USA as a 'kit of parts' and assembled at Derby. They provided luxury accommodation only and were used as parlour cars, with no catering services offered, painted in the MR's drab maroon livery.

The LBSCR introduced individual Pullman cars in its train formations from 1875 and again they only employed Parlour cars with no dinning services. The first Pullman car to run on the Brighton line is recorded as being named *Jupiter*. It was an eight-wheeled Parlour car of 28 tons and had been transferred from the Midland Railway in 1875. It was followed in 1877, by two other former Midland Railway cars of similar dimensions, which were named *Albert Edward* and *Alexandra*. Not running as a complete train, the three cars were incorporated singly into express services on the Brighton main line. Pullman cars proved to be such a success that the LBSCR signed a contract with Pullman's British subsidiary to provide Pullman restaurant cars on its Brighton expresses.

In 1878 Pullman parlour car *Victoria* returned to the Pullman shops at Derby for conversion to a dining car, and in the late summer of 1879, now renamed *Prince of Wales*, it emerged from the shops at Derby and was sent over to the Great Northern Railway. When a train which included this Pullman car included in its formation, left Leeds for King's Cross, on 1 November 1879, the GNR formally inaugurated the first British dining-car service. The Pullman car accommodated 10 First-class passengers, who each paid a supplement of two shillings and sixpence. *Prince of Wales*, which had a kitchen from which hot food was served, also included a gentlemen's smoking room and a ladies' dressing room. It was, however, the LBSCR that pioneered the running of the all-Pullman car train in England. The 'Pullman Limited Express' service which began running on 5 December 1881 consisted of four Pullman cars that had been assembled at the Pullman Car Co's workshops in Derby — *Beatrice, Louise, Maud* and *Victoria*,

The first Pullman Car to run on the Brighton Line is said to have been in 1875 and was called *Jupiter*. It was an eight-wheeled Parlour Car of twenty-eight tons. It was followed in 1877 by two other cars of similar dimensions, named *Albert Edward* and *Alexandra*. Seen near the end of its days in the late 1960s, *Albert Edward* is located at the rear of the Preston Park Pullman Works, after it had been used as a staff works canteen. (Antony M. Ford)

this last being the second Pullman car to be so named; railways have long been famous for recycling their assets, and names are no exception!

During this period all railway carriages were oil-lit when built, but over time most of them were converted either to gas (with gas tanks fitted under the floor — highly dangerous in the event of an accident, increasing the risk of fire) or the LBSCR's pioneering system of electric lighting. In 1881 William Stroudley fitted incandescent electric lighting to the stock used for the 'Pullman Limited Express', which became the first electrically lit train to run anywhere in the world. However, good though the system was, it was soon decided that

the use of dynamos run from the carriage axles would be preferable to charging the batteries each time the train arrived at the end of its journey. A change of working practice meant that only the brake coaches and vans had batteries and dynamos. The batteries were moved inside the body of the coach rather than beneath. In this method of working the electricity was supplied to the other coaches in the train

from the brake via electric cables. The 'Pullman Limited Express' service made two down and two up trips each day, with one trip each way on Sundays. Then, in 1887, the service was renamed the 'Brighton Pullman Limited', when First-class cars were included in the train's formation.

In 1888 a second all-Pullman service was instituted. The train had three newly constructed Pullman

This sign was once fitted to the wall in the far end vestibule of Pullman Car *Albert Edward* as is seen in the previous image. It was quite fortuitously removed from the Car in the 1960s, as soon afterwards this Pullman gem was set alight by vandals. Although the fire was quickly put out by the fire brigade, the car was subsequently broken up. Thankfully this sign now forms part of the author's collection. (Author)

The date of the Inaugural Run of the LBSCR's 'The Pullman Limited' was 5 December 1881, two years after the GNR. The train consisted of four renamed Pullman Cars: *Louise* (formerly *Ariel*) a Pullman Car constructed in August 1876, *Beatrice* (formerly *Globe*), *Victoria II* (formerly *Adonis*) and *Maud* (formerly *Ceres*). The new service also offered travel with electric lighting for the first time in the country. This large scale model, at a scale of 1:8, was made by employees of the Pullman Car Co. and was based on the original Pullman Car, *Louise*. The model was constructed to show how the various parts of a Pullman Car were put together. Condemned on 31 December 1929, the original *Louise* was sold in 1930 and still exists as a home at Selsey in Sussex, whilst the model now resides at the Science Museum, London. (Antony M. Ford)

Pullmann Limited, L. N. & S. C. R.

The *Brighton Limited* was introduced on 2 October 1898 and from the beginning, the new train was timed to make the journey from Victoria to Brighton in one hour. Then on 21 December 1902, the *Brighton Limited* made a record run of fifty four minutes. But the *Brighton Limited* faced the threat of a competing electric railway being introduced from London to Brighton. The challenge was taken up and the *Brighton Limited* was run to Brighton in 48 mins 41 secs, with the return to London being completed in 50 mins 21 secs, so matching the schedule put forward by the promoters of the new electric line. The image shows a contemporary view of this service, however, it is shown on the postcard as the 'Pullmann Limited, L.N.& S.C.R.' instead of 'Pullman Limited, L.B.& S.C.R.' (Author)

cars, which, as usual, had been shipped over in parts from the Pullman Palace Car Co in the USA. This time, however, the Pullman cars were assembled by the LBSCR at its Brighton Works rather than at the Pullman works in Derby. A press demonstration run of new stock for the new 'Pullman Limited' was conducted on 10 December, and on 11 December the service commenced regular operation. The train consisted of the new stock of vestibuled Pullman cars — *Albert Victor*, a parlour car, *Prince*, a buffet car, and *Princess*, a smoking car.

Ten years later, on 2 October 1898, the 'Brighton Limited' service was introduced. This ran only on Sundays and not at all during the holiday months of

July until September, but from the start, the new luxury express passenger train service was timed to make the journey from Victoria to Brighton in exactly one hour, making it possible to use the slogan 'London to Brighton in one hour' for the very first time. Then, on 21 December 1902, the 'Brighton Limited' completed a record run from Victoria to Brighton in an astonishing 54 minutes.

The 'Brighton Limited' luxury Pullman service once again hit the headlines when it was threatened with competition from a proposed new electric-powered railway between London to Brighton. The LBSCR took the challenge seriously,

In the past, train travel was quite an uncomfortable experience. So the Pullman Car Company, founded in 1880, was adopted by the LBSCR to improve its services. Here is Brighton Atlantic N° 41 heading an example of the Pullman Car standard of sumptuousness. (John Scott-Morgan)

Lawton Billinton joined the LBSCR in 1900 as an apprentice and by the end of 1907 was a Locomotive Superintendent at the New Cross Gate Works facility. In 1903, he changed the colour of the ordinary LBSCR coaches to umber brown, with white or cream upper panels. In 1906, this colour scheme was also adopted by the Pullman Car Co., together with the name of the car in large gilt letters on the lower panel and flanked on each side by a coloured transfer of the Pullman Company's crest. Here, a Marsh H1 class Atlantic is seen at Victoria Station as it departs with its train for Brighton. The train is formed of Pullman stock. (John Scott-Morgan)

When N° 422 entered service in July 1911 and shared the London - Brighton express train work with other H2 class Atlantics, including the heavily loaded Pullman services the 'Brighton Limited' and the 'Southern Belle', the LBSCR described it as 'The most luxurious train in the World'. N° 422 is seen here on one such working. (John Scott-Morgan)

and with all the stops pulled out the 'Brighton Limited' ran to Brighton in 48min 41sec, the return run to London being completed in 50min 21sec, matching the schedule promised by promoters of the new-fangled electric railway.

The Pullman colour scheme of umber (brown) and cream owed its origins to the LBSCR, for in 1903 Lawton Billinton, destined to be the railway's Locomotive, Carriage & Wagon Superintendent from 1912 until 1922, had changed the colour of its ordinary coaches to umber, with white or cream upper panels, and it was this scheme that was adopted by the Pullman Car Co in 1906. The name of each Pullman

In 1906 the LBSCR introduced three new, thirty-five ton, twelve-wheeler, Pullman Cars: *Princess Ena*, *Princess Patricia* and *Duchess of Norfolk*. These three cars were the first Pullman Cars to be painted in the new umber & cream livery. Until then, the Brighton Pullmans had been painted in a dark mahogany brown with gold lining and scrollwork. Some of the older cars had the name in an oval panel on the side. The new livery was adopted by the Pullman Car Co. in 1906. (Author)

THE LONDON, BRIGHTON, & SOUTH COAST RAILWAY

PULLMAN CAR, "DUCHESS OF NORFOLK"

Extreme length, 63′ 8½″	Carried on 6-wheel bogies, Pullman Standard.	Westinghouse brake.
,, width, 8′ 10¾″	Seating ⎰20 saloon.	Vestibules, wide open, latest type. Electric lighting.
Height from rail, 12′ 10¾″	capacity ⎱12 smoking-room	Heated by hot water system. Ventilated by revolving fans.
Inside finish, vermilion wood throughout.	Saloon revolving chairs, upholstered olive green plush.	Wilton carpets.
Ceilings, white and gold. Lavatory accom.	Smoking-room ,, ,,	dark green leather.

car was emblazoned in large gilt letters on the lower panel sides and flanked on either side by a coloured portrayal of the Pullman Car Co's coat of arms.

As part of the continuing improvements and upgrading to the Brighton line extra facilities were provided at Victoria, and the line from Earlswood to Balcombe Tunnel was widened. Upon the completion of these works a daily all-Pullman express passenger service was once again introduced.

Such was the demand for luxury travel in 1908 that a complete train of brand-new, sumptuously appointed 12-wheel Pullman cars was introduced on a daily express service between London and Brighton. On 8 November 1908 a seven-days-a-week, all-year-round service from London to Brighton commenced. Named the 'Southern Belle', the train was formed of Parlour Brake *Verona*, Parlour Buffet *Grosvenor*, Parlour cars *Cleopatra*, *Belgravia*, *Bessborough* and *Princess Helen* and Parlour Brake *Alberta*. Contemporary advertising by the LBSCR claimed that this was 'the most luxurious train in the world', and it could be experienced for a special Victoria to Brighton 'day-return' fare of 12s, which at that time with the average earnings of around £1 a week, was a premium rate ticket. By 1910, the service was increased to two trips each way running every day and later on, three services were run on Sundays. Third-class Pullman cars began running on Sunday 12 September 1915, from Victoria to Brighton and Eastbourne and the train continued to operate in this form, until it

succumbed to being replaced by electric units in 1933.

From its very beginnings the Brighton line was an innovative railway, eager to try out different forms of new technology and different modes of working to provide its passengers a fast and efficient train service. Among these was the practice of 'slipping', whereby a train on the move would detach one or more vehicles under the control of a separate guard, enabling the railway to increase the number of destinations served by a single train. The earliest instance of slipping was to be found in 1840 on the cable-worked London & Blackwall Railway, and experiments with locomotive-hauled trains are known to have been conducted in the mid-1850s. However, it was the LBSCR's successful slipping of the Hastings portion of a London–Brighton express, at Haywards Heath in February 1858, that attracted the attention of the wider

railway community, and by 1914 there were some 176 slips daily nationwide. One example on the LBSCR was the 8.45am departure from Brighton, which served both of the railway's London termini — London Bridge and Victoria. The

Pullman Car *Princess Margaret* was originally an American-built Pullman Car, constructed in March 1893. It ran in this form on the LBSCR and was rebuilt as a Kitchen Car at Longhedge Works in June 1913, where it received twenty-four seats. It was rebuilt again, but this time the London and South Western Railway turned it into an eight-wheel Parlour Car. It was finally condemned in June 1932. (Antony M. Ford)

Contemporary advertising by the LBSCR, claimed that the '*Southern Belle*' was '... the most luxurious train in the world...' In 1908 this could be experienced for a special Victoria to Brighton day return fare of 12 shillings. (Author)

The Maximum of Luxury
at the Minimum of Cost.

"PULLMAN" and "PERFECTION"

are synonyms when they refer to Car Building, in which art the Pullman Car Company leads the world. In elaborate design, substantial construction, and luxurious finish, Pullman Cars represent the highest standard of excellence.

Ingenuity and skill are constantly being applied to the improvement of details with a view to adding to the comfort of travel. Every Car is in charge of an experienced well-trained Conductor, whose services are always at hand from start to finish of a journey, and invalids and ladies with children can always rely upon ready attention to their comfort and convenience.

Cleanliness is also a special feature, coupled with perfect ventilation and good lighting, thus making travelling a real luxury.

Pullman Drawing Room, Buffet, Dining, and Observation Cars are in operation on the following important lines :—

Southern Railway :
L. B. & S. C. Section ; Victoria and London Bridge to Brighton, Hove, Worthing, Eastbourne, Bognor, Newhaven, Portsmouth, &c.

S. E. & C. Section : Victoria and Charing Cross to Dover and Folkestone in all the Continental Services. Also Deal, Ramsgate, Margate, and Kent Coast Towns.

London and North Eastern Railway :
Gt. Eastern Section : Buffet Cars (First and Third Class) between Liverpool Street and principal stations, also First and Second Class on Continental Trains.

London Midland and Scottish Railway :
Caledonian Section ; Glasgow & Edinburgh to Aberdeen, Oban, Perth, Stirling, Gleneagles, Dumblane, Forfar, Callander, Lockerbie, Loch Awe, Carstairs, Beattock, Carlisle, &c.

Highland Section ; Blair Atholl, Newtonmore, Kingussie, Kincraig, Aviemore, &c.

Metropolitan Railway : Buffet Cars are run between Aldgate, Liverpool Street, Baker Street, Aylesbury, Chesham, and Verney Junction.

Observation Car, "MAID OF MORVEN"

"The Southern Belle"
The most Luxurious Train in the World.

Daily (including Sundays). Pullman Train de Luxe. Running between LONDON AND BRIGHTON.

THIRD CLASS "PULLMAN" CARS between LONDON, BRIGHTON, EASTBOURNE, PORTSMOUTH, &c.

Refreshments. Breakfasts, Luncheons, Teas, Suppers, and other refreshments can be obtained on the Cars.

Reservations. Reservations can be effected through the Station Superintendents at the various termini, either by letter, telegram, or telephone.

Special Facilities. Cars for private parties can be specially reserved, under certain conditions, upon application to the various Railway Companies.

The Pullman Car Company, Limited,
Chief London Office—

VICTORIA STATION (S. E. & C. R.), PIMLICO, S.W.1.
Telegraphic Address—"Pullman, Phone, London." Telephone No.—Victoria 9978 (2 lines)
Branch Office—CENTRAL STATION (Caledonian Railway), GLASGOW.
Telephone No.—Central 7473.
Thomas Powell, Secretary and Manager.

An advertisement from the Railway Year Book of 1924 shows the Pullman Car Company's 'Pullman and Perfection' of the LBSCR's 'Southern Belle' service from London to Brighton. (Author)

practice was to include a Pullman car in each of the portions to serve breakfast to the passengers. The Victoria portion was slipped at East Croydon and, having coasted to a halt, was coupled to a locomotive which then hauled it to Victoria. The evening service returned at 5pm. The service was so popular that it was named as the 'City Limited', its prestige being such that in 1907 Albert Panter, Manager for Carriage & Wagon Construction

at Brighton, produced a new nine-coach train set specifically for it. The two Pullman cars used for this service were taken off in the First World War and never reinstated.

Two other slipped Pullman services ran on the Brighton line, both in the down direction, both slips being effected at Haywards Heath. Perusing the LBSCR's timetables one soon realises that timetable revisions were an ever-present feature of the railway operations in pre-First World War days. It is in the introductory pages of the timetable commencing on October 1908 that we encounter these slip workings. But the 10am departure also included a slip portion for Brighton, which comprised five vehicles, including a Pullman car, and in the same 1908 timetable alterations we find a 3.35pm departure from Victoria to Brighton and West Worthing, with Pullman cars included in both portions. Once again the Haywards Heath passengers were served by gliding gently to a stop in the designated section. The practice of slipping coaches on the Brighton line was abolished in April 1932 with the advent of electrification.

Over the years motive power improved considerably, from R. J. Billinton's 4-4-0s, through Marsh's H1 and H2 Atlantics, to L. B. Billinton's Baltic tanks. After the Grouping came Maunsell 2-6-4Ts and 2-6-0s and finally 'King Arthur' 4-6-0s, a number of which were built especially for the Brighton line's prestige Pullman services.

The 'Southern Belle' was so successful that when the Brighton line was electrified in 1933 the steam-hauled stock used hitherto

was replaced by electric multiple-units composed entirely of Pullman stock. A normal working would comprise two of the three five-car units, forming a 10-car train. Provided First- and Third-class accommodation for Pullman travellers, it became the world's first all-Pullman electric train service.

On the LBSCR's Pullman 'slip' services, a separate guard was needed for each coach or portion of train that was 'slipped'. This usually took place at East Croydon for up services or Haywards Heath for the down services. (Author)

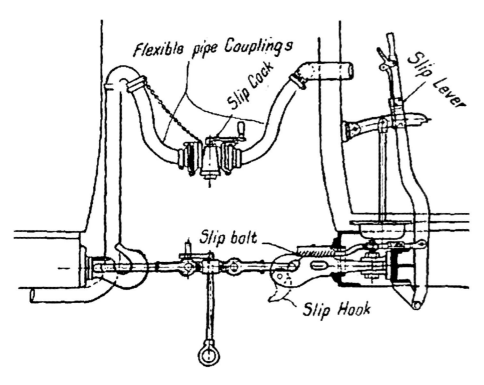

In this view the slip guard is looking out of his window at the end of the slip coach, after he has operated the slip lever to separate his coach from the rest of the train. He would then use the brake lever, seen immediately to his right, to bring the slipped coach to a safe and smooth stop. It was, of course, up to the slip guard to judge when to operate the mechanism according to the speed of the train and prevailing weather conditions. Once the slipped coach had come to a complete standstill, a locomotive would come along and shunt the coach onto another train, allowing it to continue to its planned destination. (Author)

This diagram shows the mechanism of the slip-lever. When the guard pulled back on the lever, the bolt that kept the slip hook closed moved, thus releasing the slip hook and allowing the two coaches to separate. Also shown is the method of uniting the vacuum brake couplings so that when they were pulled apart they would operate in such a way so as to preserve a seal and so maintained a full vacuum in the braking system. (Author)

Scheduled to take 60 minutes for the non-stop 51-mile journey, it initially retained the name of its steam-hauled predecessor, but on 29 June 1934 it was formally renamed as the 'Brighton Belle', in which guise it would become world-famous. During the Second World War the service was suspended, with the '5-BEL' units being placed in store, but it was reinstated in 1946. For much of the 1950s the unit not in regular use on the Brighton service was used for a Sunday Pullman train from Eastbourne known as the 'Eastbourne Pullman', although this was discontinued in 1957. The three '5-BEL' electric units were refurbished during 1955, but by 1972 they were starting to show their age and offered a poor ride in comparison with more modern stock. Despite protests a decision was taken not to replace them, the cost being deemed too high, and the service was withdrawn on 30 April 1972.

Almost all of the '5-BEL' Pullman cars have been preserved, some of them earning their keep on the British Pullman service of the Venice Simplon Orient Express, and some are being refurbished to fulfil a widely held ambition to have a complete five-car set running again

The cover of the LBSCR's timetable for June to September 1912. (Author)

in order to re-create the 'Brighton Belle'.

To accommodate the increased number of Pullman cars on the

MAIN LINE.
HASTINGS, ST. LEONARDS, BEXHILL, EASTBOURNE, SEAFORD, LEWES, WORTHING, HOVE and BRIGHTON to LONDON.

EASTBOURNE, HEATHFIELD, MAYFIELD AND TUNBRIDGE WELLS.
Service of Trains from Eastbourne to Tunbridge Wells, showing connections FROM Londno at Polegate, and TO London at Groombridge.

Page 20 from the LBSCR's timetable for June to September 1912, showing the 'slip' detail's for Pullman services to London Bridge and Victoria. (Author)

Enlargements of the relevant sections from LBSCR's timetable for June to September 1912, detailing the Pullman 'slip' service into London Bridge and Victoria. (Author)

Brighton line the original paint shop of Brighton Works, built in the late 1880s, was taken over in 1928 by the Pullman Car Co. This building, near Preston Park, was situated within the triangle of the London–Brighton main line, the coast line west to Hove and the Prestonville Spur linking the two, adjacent to Highcroft Villas and just north of Lovers' Walk depot. Conversions, repairs and overhauls of the bodywork on all of the country's Pullman cars were carried out there. Regular jobs carried out there included the pickling, polishing and re-varnishing of the cast brass table lamps and luggage racks, along with the French-polishing of the intricate marquetry panels.

The Pullman Car Co's new workshops at Preston Park, Brighton, opened on 5 December 1928, replacing facilities that had been located at Longhedge since 1912. Longhedge Works then became the Pullman Car Co's commissary depot. In November 1963 the Pullman workshops at Preston Park finally closed in the wake of the Beeching cuts, with the loss of some 100 jobs and countless irreplaceable skills, Pullman

maintenance being transferred to other railway workshops. At the time of closure of the Pullman works at Preston Park, the Pullman company and its workshops, offices and facilities were absorbed by the British Railway Board.

Following closure of the Pullman works the building was used for some time to store preserved steam and diesel locomotives, goods wagons and coaches, including a number of former 'Brighton Belle' cars, and from time to time some of these items would be exhibited at open days held at Brighton station. In due course the decision was taken to demolish the Pullman Works building, so on Sunday 7 September 2008 an intricate plan was put into action to remove the items of historic rolling stock stored

The B4 class 4-4-0s were used for express passenger work on the LBSCR. They were designed by R. J. Billinton and were either built at Brighton Works between 1899–1902 or by Messrs Sharp, Stewart and Co in 1901. The B4 class successfully worked the heaviest express trains on the LBSCR until around 1912, when they were gradually replaced by the larger H1, H2, J1 & J2 classes. Thereafter they were regularly used on slower and lighter services. According to O. S. Nock, the B4 class '... were among the finest passenger locomotives of their day.' Here is Nº 70 *Holyrood* as it appeared circa 1910. (Author)

within. Thanks to this £110,000 exercise, 11 items of stock were re-housed at the Swanage, Colne Valley and Bluebell preservation sites. The gem in terms of carriage stock was undoubtedly the body of Pullman sleeper car *Balmoral*, which went for restoration. Built in 1882 in Detroit and shipped to Derby for assembly, the coach was taken out of service in 1907, following which its body apparently remained hidden away at Brighton for more than a century.

Pullman cars were long a favourite aspect of services linking London and Brighton — so much so that they became the trademark of the line, be they steam-hauled or electric. It is, therefore, pleasing to be able to report that some of the original Brighton-line cars are being restored to working order, to allow passengers to relive the grandeur and the glory of the 'Brighton Belle'.

Car Nº 86 is a third class Parlour Trailer Car, built in 1933 for '*Brighton Belle*' unit Nº 2051, which later became Nº 3051. The all-electric '*Brighton Belle*' units replaced the steam hauled '*Southern Belle*' train. Nº 86 seated fifty-six passengers in a four-bay and a three-bay saloon configuration with a central divider. It had a lavatory, vestibule and a corridor connection at each end. (Antony M. Ford)

On its formation in 1923, the Southern Railway took over and renewed the original 1877 contract between the LBSCR and the Pullman Car Company. When the SR electrified its main line to Brighton, Pullman provided restaurant cars for the new express electric-powered multiple units. A special fleet of three five-car all-Pullman units to operate the 'Southern Belle' service were built and the service was renamed the 'Brighton Belle' in 1934. Here we see unit Nº 3051 and its fellow classmates, in the corporate livery of blue and grey, resting between duties at Brighton's electric depot. The units were all withdrawn from service, with the last 'Brighton Belle' service running on Sunday, 30 April 1972. (Antony M. Ford)

A circa 1962 birds-eye view, looking north towards Preston Park, of the Pullman Workshops and adjoining lines. The cars on the immediate left are all K-Type and to the right is a 6PUL electric unit. (Antony M. Ford)

Car Nº 74 inside Preston Park workshops, flanked by two conventional K-Type Cars. Details to note in the foreground are the carpenters benches with partially finished tables and a chair frame on the right. (Antony M. Ford / Courtesy Joe Kent)

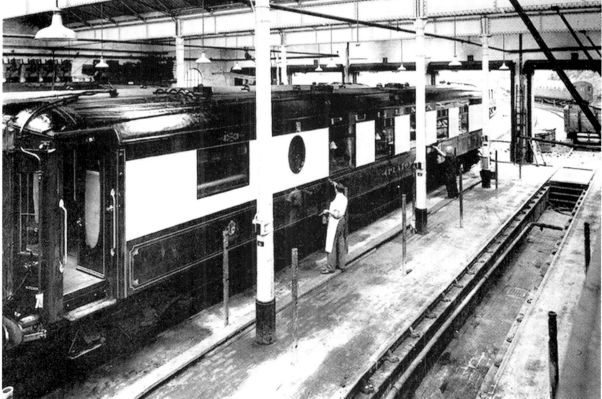

A view of Preston Park Workshops in 1959, with painters putting the finishing touches to Pullman Car - *Plato* (11). (Antony M. Ford)

Pullman Cars have always been synonymous with the Brighton Line. This magnificent collection of Pullman ephemera and memorabilia celebrates the glory of a former mode of transport that has sadly been swept away from the Brighton Line due to modernisation. (Author) (Courtesy of The Brighton Toy & Model Museum, Brighton)

Chapter 9

THE H1 ATLANTICS

Coming from the Great Northern Railway, Douglas Earle Marsh fully appreciated the worth of the H. A. Ivatt-designed large-boiler Atlantics, having been involved in their very design. Thus it was that when a class of powerful, fast express locomotives were needed on the Brighton line, he had the perfect answer and had no hesitation in following this revolutionary design. Marsh obtained a full set of drawings from Doncaster Works and made the necessary modifications, marked in red ink. Once approved, the drawings were sent to Kitson & Co, Leeds, in April 1905 for five examples to be constructed. The original contract price of £3,950 for each locomotive and tender was later reduced by £45, after Marsh had written to Kitson requesting that the locomotives be delivered in grey primer instead of Stroudley's yellow livery.

It would be December 1905 before the first locomotive arrived in Brighton territory, some three

When the LBSCR ordered five new Atlantic passenger express locomotives from Kitson & Co, the original contract price was £3,950 for each of the five engines and their tenders. However, the price was later reduced by £45 after D. E. Marsh had written to Kitson & Co (Leeds), requesting that the locomotives be delivered in grey primer and not having a top coat of paint. It was normal for engines to be run-in in their primer as adjustments may have been likely and they would have received their top coat after about 1,000 miles had been clocked up. Here, Nº 37 is seen shortly after receiving its coat of Marsh Umber paint. (John Scott-Morgan)

The LBSCR's 4-4-2 Atlantic locomotive N° 38 was delivered on 24 December 1905 and was assigned to Brighton Shed. (John Scott-Morgan)

The LBSCR's 4-4-2 Atlantic locomotive N° 38 is seen here with a passenger service from East Grinstead to London as it passes over Riddlesdown Viaduct. (John Scott-Morgan)

months late, the delivery dates being as follows:

N° 37 10 December 1905

N° 38 24 December 1905, assigned to Brighton depot in the care of Driver William Vallance

N° 39 23 January 1906

N° 40 2 February 1906, assigned to Brighton depot in the care of Driver George Pont

N° 41 19 February 1906, assigned to Brighton depot in the care of Driver John Tompsett

From the beginning of the Stroudley era the LBSCR numbered all of its boilers in ascending order, the list including all boilers built for the railway by outside contractors.

When they first entered traffic

N°s 37, 38 and 39, appeared in the LBSCR's official locomotive register as Class B5, but by the time N°s 40 and 41 were delivered in February 1906 the classification had been altered to 'H', which on 1 January 1907 would be changed again, to H1.

Interestingly the coupled wheels were of 6ft 7½in diameter, exactly the same as on the GNR design. The boiler, 5ft 6in in diameter and with a firebox 5ft 1in wide, was far larger than anything the Brighton company had previously built. The class differed from the GNR's 'Large Atlantics' in that the firebox was deeper, but it had the same grate area and had the working pressure fixed at 200lb in place of 175lb. Cylinder sizes differed between

The LBSCR's 4-4-2 Atlantic locomotive N° 39 is seen here festooned with Royal train locomotive regalia. (John Scott-Morgan)

When D. E. Marsh's Atlantic express passenger locomotives first entered traffic in the LBSCR's official Locomotive Register, N° 37, N° 38 and N° 39 were shown as B5 class, which was the next available class in this category. However, when N° 40 and N° 41 were delivered in February 1906, the classification was altered to H Atlantic class and on 1 January 1907 it was changed again to H1 class, which was then retained until the withdrawal of the class. Here N° 39 is seen on a Pullman car express, on the Brighton main line. (John Scott-Morgan)

D. E. Marsh's Atlantic express passenger locomotive N° 39, fitted with an indicator shield, is seen here in this posed image. (John Scott-Morgan)

individual locomotives; 18½x26in cylinders were fitted to N°s 37, 38 and 40, whereas N°s 39 and 41 had cylinders of 19in diameter. The Brighton Atlantics had a longer piston stroke compared with the GNR locomotives, which had 18¾x24in cylinders.

The Brighton Atlantics were lively locomotives and were good on acceleration, even with heavy loads. Apart from the changes in the cylinder dimensions, the cylinders used the same working design as the GNR version, whereby flat valves were housed in the steam-chests between the frames and they exhausted straight through the rear of the blast-pipe. This was a good free arrangement which permitted the best use being made of the steam supply.

A 1,000-mile running-in period was completed before the new umber livery was applied, with gold lining-out, although initially the wheel-splashers were devoid of any other embellishments. At the first repaint, the splashers were decorated with the LBSCR's company monogram, formed of the LBSCR's intertwined initials, in such complicated form that they 'overflowed' with pointed embellishments and were given the nickname of 'raspberries'. Eventually Lawson Billinton, who was caretaker for D. E. Marsh whilst he was on leave of absence due to ill health, discarded them in favour of a coat of arms.

Fuel consumption of the H1s

D. E. Marsh's Atlantic express passenger locomotive N° 39 is seen with a 'Southern Belle' as it approaches Purley Station. The vehicle immediately behind the tender looks like a shortened Pullman Car and was known affectionately as a 'Pullman Pup'. It was in fact nothing more than a baggage car which had been constructed and painted to resemble a full size car. (John Scott-Morgan)

SOUTHERN BELLE L·B·S·C·RY

The LBSCR pioneered the running of all Pullman Car trains in England when the inaugural 'Pullman Limited Express' began on 5 December 1881. It consisted of four Pullman Cars, which had been assembled at the Pullman Car Company workshops in Derby: Beatrice, Louise, Maud and Victoria. At that time all carriages were oil-lit, but most were converted either to gas (with gas tanks under the carriages) or the LBSCR system of electric lighting. In 1881, William Stroudley fitted incandescent electric lighting to the 'Pullman Limited Express' rolling stock using Faure cells, making it the first train in the world to be lit by electricity. Here the 'Pullman Limited Express' is seen being worked by the fourth Brighton Atlantic; N° 40. (Author)

Marsh Atlantic N° 39 is seen running at 'full pelt' with an express working. (John Scott-Morgan)

Here the crisp, clean, elegant lines of the front end of fourth Brighton Atlantic (N° 40) are shown to good effect. (John Scott-Morgan)

and H2s was lower than that of the B4 4-4-0s on similar duties but exceeded that of the I3 4-4-2Ts, for, good as they were, the tank engines were quite outclassed in terms of performance, particularly acceleration. The almost 38 tons of adhesion and the efficient steam sanding gear on the H1s and H2s gave the footplate crews the confidence and opportunity of putting the large free-steaming boilers to good use. A possible weakness was their propensity to stop at dead-centre which would cause delays on restarting, unless the grade was favourable. No satisfactory reason was ever found and the later H2 Atlantics never seemed to suffer as badly.

Despite the short coupled wheelbase and large outside cylinders the running was apparently remarkably smooth, this being attributable to the use of Timmis spiral springing on the bogie and driving wheels but also of the Doncaster swing-link bogie, which was also used and gave long

and satisfactory service on Marsh's 4-4-2Ts (Classes I1, I2, I3, and I4) and 4-6-2Ts (Classes J1 and J2).

Another difference between Brighton and Doncaster Atlantics lay in the distance behind the trailing axle, the Marsh locomotives having an extra 15¾in, which allowed for a larger cab. However, this was probably due to the use of a screw-reversing mechanism rather than a lever, which may have forced the issue. Further differences between the LBSCR and GNR locomotives included a deeper Wootten-style firebox, square cabs with the roof supported by the rear pillars, Billinton Derby-pattern chimneys, neater safety valves, the curving of the running plate both over the cylinders and the coupled wheels, bogie fitted brakes, Westinghouse air brakes and the fitting of a Brighton-style tender.

The arrangement of the Stephenson valve gear was similar to that used on the Doncaster Atlantics, with the expansion link placed behind the leading coupled axle and the intermediate valve spindle, which was sited forward of the link and curved upwards to clear that axle. The coupling-rod cranks had a throw of 12in, but that of the connecting-rod pins was 13in, for these were turned off-centre with the coupling rod pins. Another unusual feature was the method employed to secure the tyres to the wheels, this being achieved by means of set-pins placed between each pair of spokes and not, as was usual, between alternate pairs.

The boilers, which like their Doncaster equivalents steamed magnificently, were made of steel in two rings, the firebox, of the

D. E. Marsh's 4-4-2 Atlantic Nº 39 is seen at Brighton Station waiting to depart with a working to London Bridge. (John Scott-Morgan)

Marsh's Atlantic Nº 40 enters Platform 5 at East Croydon with a down stopping service from London Bridge or Willow Walk to Brighton, via Redhill. (John Scott-Morgan)

modified Wootten type, having the grate resting on the main frames. There were two Ramsbottom-type safety valves located over the firebox and they were contained in a typical Doncaster flat-sided casing. The Westlinghouse pump was placed between the frames ahead of the smokebox, with the live and exhaust steam pipe passing externally below it. The smokebox, following Billinton practice, was double-skinned, which undoubtedly kept the external paintwork in good repair, albeit at the expense of maintenance complications. From 1920 all smokebox renewals were of single metal sheeting but made to the same diameter as the original double-skinned pattern.

The last member of D. E. Marsh's 4-4-2 Atlantics to be delivered in this batch was Nº 41, delivered on 19 February 1906. It was assigned to Brighton Shed in the care of Driver John Tompsett. It is seen at Victoria Station departing with the 'Southern Belle' to Brighton. (John Scott-Morgan)

When new Nºs 37, 38 and 39 were fitted with short cab roofs, even though the cab was larger than on the GNR locomotives, but following complaints of inadequate protection Nºs 40 and 41 entered service with lengthened roofs. No change was made to the first three locomotives until after the Grouping, when Maunsell extended their roofs to match those of Nºs 40

and 41, giving the fireman greater protection when removing coal from the tender. When delivered Nº 37 also had other differences from the rest of the batch, notably in having the builder's plates attached to the framing ahead of the smokebox using snap-head (instead of countersunk) rivets; when it was repainted in umber livery these plates were moved to a position

ahead of the leading coupled wheels, where they had been from the outset on the other H1s. After the Grouping Maunsell arranged for the entire class to receive alterations for the locomotives to conform to the composite loading gauge, giving them a wider route availability. They were also superheated, bringing them into line with the later H2s.

All five H1s were based at Brighton, and after being run in on slow and semi-fast duties they were set to work on the most arduous main-line expresses of the day, including the prestige Pullman services. Of the latter, the 'Sunday Pullman Limited' was the best known, and following its introduction in 1881 it seldom ran with empty accommodation, even in the depths of winter. A 60min schedule was first operated in 1898, and it was to this timing that H1 N° 39 covered the 50.9 miles from Victoria to Brighton in 51min 48sec, on 30 June 1907. Although hampered by permanent-way checks it managed the seven-mile climb of 1 in 264 from Horley to Balcombe at over 60mph and achieved 86½mph near Wivelsfield with a load of five eight-wheeled Pullman cars, two 12-wheeled

When H1 class Atlantics N° 37, N° 38 and N° 39 were originally built they were fitted with short cab roofs, but following complaints of inadequate protection to footplate crew, N° 40 and N° 41 entered service with lengthened roofs. No change was made to the first three locomotives before the grouping, when the roofs of all five locomotives were arranged to be the same length, giving fireman reasonable protection when removing coal from the tender. As N° 40, waits to depart, we see that the fireman is leaning over to reach the coal and that the cab roof extends out towards the tender. (Author)

Nº 37 differed from the rest of the batch when delivered as it had the makers plates attached to the framing just behind the smokebox, and was attached using snap headed instead of countersunk rivets to the valance in front of the cylinders. When Nº 37 was painted into umber livery, the plates on Nº 37 were moved to a position ahead of the leading coupled wheels. Here we see Nº 37 with its builder's plate in the same position as the rest of the class. (Author)

ATLANTIC EXPRESS LOCOMOTIVE. LONDON BRIGHTON & SOUTH COAST RAILWAY.

The Sunday Pullman Limited was the best known prestige service on the Brighton Line and since its introduction in 1881, it seldom ran with empty accommodation even in the depths of winter. A sixty minute schedule was first operated in 1898 and it was to this timing that Nº 39 ran the 50.9 miles from Victoria to Brighton in 51 mins 48 secs on 30 June 1907. This contemporary cigarette card shows the famed locomotive. (Author)

Pullman cars and two six-wheeled vans, giving a total tare weight of 228 tons 14cwt. By this time, however, the rival electric schemes had faded away, and the LBSCR settled down to its normal 60min schedule.

With effect from 1 November 1908 the 'Sunday Pullman Limited' service was replaced by the 'Southern Belle', for which Pullman cars *Verona, Princess Helen, Belgravia, Grosvenor, Cleopatra, Bessborough* and *Alberta* were specially constructed at a cost of £5,950. All of the Pullman cars, which had an empty weight of 40 tons, were luxuriously appointed and were carried on two six-wheeled bogies. The new Pullman-car service made two journeys in each direction on Sundays to the 60min schedule; from 1 June 1909 similar facilities were made available on weekdays. From the start the H1 Atlantics were regularly associated with the workings, Nº 39 being accorded the honour of working the inaugural train, accomplishing the task in 58min 18sec. During the winter months, when the full train formation was deemed unnecessary (other than at weekends), it was usual for the surplus Pullman cars to earn their keep on other London express services. Two cars, for instance, together with an example of an earlier vintage of Pullman cars, were included in the formation of the 8.45am ex-Brighton service, making this one of the heaviest loaded workings on the Brighton line. For 1909/10 the train's total weight was 392 tons 10cwt, formed as follows:

Nº 48 Third-class carriage
(23 tons 0cwt)
Nº 168 Third-class carriage
(23 tons 15cwt)
Nº 165 First-class brake carriage
(25 tons 10cwt)
Nº 163 First-class carriage
(27 tons 0cwt)
Nº 161 First-class carriage
(28 tons 10cwt)
Belgravia First-class carriage
(40 tons 0cwt)
Grosvenor First-class carriage
(40 tons 0cwt)
Nº 151 First-class carriage
(27 tons 0cwt)
Nº 152 First-class carriage
(26 tons 5cwt)
Nº 31 First-class brake carriage
(26 tons 10cwt)
Nº 166 First-class brake carriage
(25 tons 10cwt)
Princess Eva First-class carriage
(32 tons 10cwt)
Nº 162 First-class carriage
(27 tons 0cwt)
Nº 85 First-class carriage
(20 tons 0cwt)

At East Croydon the last four cars in the formation were slipped for Victoria, the remainder of the train continuing to London Bridge. This latter portion, having had the two Third-class carriages removed, then formed the 5pm London Bridge–Brighton service, the train's weight now being 240 tons — considerably lighter than the 8.45am up working.

When new Nºs 37 and 38 were plagued with overheating trailing axleboxes, but once this was overcome the class as a whole seldom spent much time out of traffic and during the period 1906-9 they ran high mileages, as shown in the accompanying table. Nº 39, was always considered to be a 'good

LAMBERT & BUTLER'S 'CIGARETTES.

LONDON, BRIGHTON & SOUTH COAST RY. LOCOMOTIVE 39.

engine' and as such was reserved for Royal and other important duties. It was in this capacity that it worked the train that conveyed King George V to Portsmouth, for the Coronation Naval Review on 24 June 1911.

Marsh abandoned the Brighton practice of naming passenger locomotives, and as a result only one of the 'H1s' bore a name during LBSCR days, N° 39 being named *La France* in June 1913, prior to working the train carrying the French President, Raymond Poincaré, to Portsmouth. This name was carried until January 1926, when it was renamed by the Southern Railway as *Hartland Point*.

When the locomotives were new the Westinghouse air-brake system applied brake shoes to all wheel-sets on the locomotive and tender, but the bogie brakes were found to be more trouble than they were worth and were discarded in period 1914-16. Steam heating for the passenger stock was fitted to all five locomotives in October 1908 at Brighton, either on shed or (in the case of N° 40) in works. Then, during March 1914, commencing with N° 40, the Robert Billinton-Derby chimneys were replaced with a cast-iron pattern similar to that carried by the H2 Atlantics. At the same time N° 40 lost its smooth-sided Doncaster safety-valve casing, receiving the standard flared variety. But whereas the chimneys had been changed by November 1919 (the last to retain the earlier pattern being N° 38), the original safety-valve casing was still carried by N° 37 when it was first painted in Southern Railway green during August 1924, finally being

Location	Regulator opening %	Cut-off %	Boiler pressure/ sq. in	Speed	Horse Power
Leaving Victoria	75	40	200	14	789.8
Grosvenor Bank Box	75	40	200	27	1,183.9
Wandsworth Bank	75	40	181	49	1,327.3
Balham Junction	50	45	170	50	1,124.1
Thornton Heath	50	50	180	55	1,263.7
East Croydon	50	45	195	56	1,249.2
Purley	50	45	182	55	1,381.2
Stoats Nest	50	50	170	53	1,402.4
Star Lane Box	50	50	183	54	1,088.9
Horley	50	50	164	55	1,208.7
Three Bridges	Full open	45	168	66	1,009.2
Balcombe	Full open	45	161	59	1,280.5
Ouse Viaduct	50	45	163	70½	1,186.3
Haywards Heath	50	45	164	78	1,205.8
Burgess Hill	Full open	45	130	73	1,123.1
Hassocks	Full open	45	130	65	989.7
Preston Park	-	-	-	-	-
Brighton	-	-	-	-	-

Here are the timings of the historic run from Victoria to Brighton on 30 June 1907 when H1 class Atlantic N° 39 ran the 50.9 miles in 51 mins 48 secs. (Author)

On 1 November 1908 the 'Southern Belle' service replaced the 'Sunday Pullman Limited' for which eight new Pullman Cars were specially constructed at a cost of £5,950. All of the Pullman Cars were luxuriously appointed and were carried on 2 six-wheeled bogies. The new Pullman Cars made two journeys in each direction on Sundays to the sixty minute schedule. Here we see the new Pullman train being worked by a member of the H1 class 4-4-2 Atlantics. (Author)

When first built H1 class Atlantics N° 37 and N° 38 were plagued with overheating trailing axle-boxes, but once this was overcome the class as a whole seldom spent much time out of traffic and ran-up many miles between 1906 and 1909. Here, a H1 class member N° 37 working a prestige Pullman service has been stopped at Balham Intermediate signal box for a posed photograph. Notice the Inspector standing in the four-foot of the up-fast line and that the engine is blowing off its safety valves. (Author)

H1 class Atlantic N° 39 is seen in LBSCR days with a Pullman Car incorporated singly into a main line London and Brighton express. (Author)

discarded in March 1926, when the locomotive was superheated and given the name *Selsey Bill*.

No spare boilers were available until April 1913, when a new boiler (N° 1000) was constructed at Brighton Works (at a cost of £1,390) and fitted to N° 39, which was then undergoing repairs. It was subsequently fitted to N°s 39 (in August 1921), 37 (October 1924), 41 (June 1927), 2039 again (July 1935), 2041 (July 1938) and 2039 for a third time (October 1942). Given a new firebox in July 1927 (when it was also superheated) and again in July 1938, the boiler was finally broken up at Brighton during January 1952.

Other changes of note included the provision of an additional Roscue lubricator for N° 38, in November 1919, and of oscillation-recorder equipment for N° 41, in January 1922. The latter spent two weeks working a wide variety of expresses and then several days running light-engine between Bognor Regis and Victoria before the equipment was removed and transferred to I3 4-4-2T N° 26, in March 1922.

During May 1920 Lawson Billinton sought permission to fit the H1s with Schmidt superheaters, at an estimated cost of £2,585, but this was refused by the Locomotive Committee, despite the promise of recouping the outlay within 18 months as a result of more efficient working. A similar request at the same meeting to superheat the saturated I3 Atlantic tanks was also rejected. It was therefore left to the Southern Railway to undertake this essential improvement after Grouping in 1923. In later years R. E. L. Maunsell fitted his own pattern of superheater to many of the Brighton locomotives that had the Schmidt or Robinson variety. Those locomotives carrying a Maunsell-designed superheater were noticeable by the pair of smokebox fitted 'snifting valves', although these were removed by O. V. S. Bulleid after the Second World War.

On 18 January 1923 N° 37 was fitted, at the expense of the manufacturer, with a Davies & Metcalf Type F exhaust-steam injector, after which it was used on the following workings, for a period of three months:

8.20am Brighton–West Worthing (light-engine)

9.38am West Worthing–Victoria

1.03pm Victoria–Brighton

6.05pm Brighton–Victoria

10.00pm Victoria–Brighton

At the end of the trial period the inspector in charge of the testing reported that the injector fell below the required delivery rate, was temperamental and wasted about 200 gallons of water per day, compared with the 30-35 gallons lost by the company's standard model. It was removed in May 1923.

During April 1923 No 41 was fitted with a pair of direct-loaded safety valves without a casing. These were of B. K. Field design and were also employed on a number of 'B4X' rebuilds, but they proved unreliable in service and were removed at an early date. Those on N° 41 gave way to the standard Ramsbottom arrangement in March 1925.

In 1925 the SR Publicity Department at Waterloo decided that named express locomotives would create an interest among travellers on the line, as well as providing an inexpensive source of advertising. Thus over the next few years all new passenger locomotives were named, as were existing machines, the latter category including the H1 and H2 Atlantics. The nameplates were of brass with neat raised lettering and red background, they were curved to fit the driving splashers and were named after South Coast landmarks. N° 39, already named *La France*, was renamed *Hartland Point* in January 1926. Later in the decade the five H1

H1 class Atlantic N° 41 in its LBSC days. Notice the LBSC coat of arms on the wheel splashers; affectionately known as a 'raspberry'. (John Scott-Morgan)

H1 class Atlantic N° 41 is seen with a train of Pullman Cars supplemented with ordinary stock as it passes through South Croydon Station on the main line to Brighton. (John Scott-Morgan)

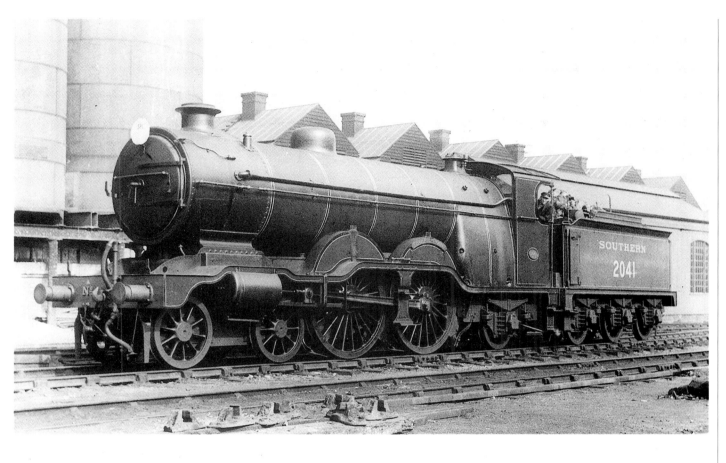

H1 class Atlantic N° 2041 is seen in Southern days at Brighton depot. The engine is in Southern lined green livery. (John Scott-Morgan)

Marsh had abandoned the Brighton practice of naming locomotives and as a result, only one of the H1s bore a name during LBSC days. H1 class Atlantic N° 39 was named *La France* and is seen here bedecked in bunting and garlands for the 1913 visit of the French President - the coal is also painted white. After the event the locomotive kept its name until January 1926, at which time the Southern Railway renamed it *Hartland Point*. (Author)

Brighton Atlantics N° 40 and N° 41, were renumbered by the Southern Railway (SR) in 1925 and became N° 2040 and N° 2041. They were withdrawn by the SR in 1944 and were the first members of the class to be so. Here we see N° 40 in happier times, working an express passenger service in LBSCR days. (Author)

Atlantics, which since the Grouping had been identified as B37-41, were renumbered as 2037-41. With the electrification of the Brighton line in 1933 their future was in doubt, but they remained at work on the Central Section and continued to perform very impressively, although Nos 2040 and 2041 were withdrawn in 1944.

On 15 January 1945 — before the cessation of hostilities — H1 N° 2038 *Portland Bill* had the distinction of working the first civilian 'Continental Express' to leave London since the withdrawal of Allied troops from France in 1940, the Channel crossing being dictated by tides pending repair of the war-damaged harbour at Dieppe. The summer of 1947 saw N° 2038 (along with H2s N°s 2422/3/6) based at Newhaven for the heavy boat trains, which had regained their pre-war popularity; this was a duty the Atlantics performed particularly well, although assistance was occasionally provided by Battersea-based U1 2-6-0s. Together with H2 N° 2421, Brighton-allocated N°s 2037 *Selsey Bill* and 2039 *Hartland Point* shared the 8.18am Uckfield–Victoria and 6.10pm return

During July 1947 N° 2039 was taken to Brighton Works for the fitting of 'sleeve' valve gear, before being employed as a mobile test-bed for O. V. S. Bulleid's proposed 'Leader'-class locomotives. It emerged on 5 November, having been fitted with new cylinders, outside steam pipes, a multiple-jet blast-pipe and a fabricated chimney; the Westinghouse air pump was mounted on the right-hand side of the smokebox, and the running plate had been cut away in the vicinity of the cylinders. A number of test runs were then made between Brighton and Lewes, and after modifications had been made to the valve gear an ex-SECR three-coach set was used on several runs to Eastbourne and back, stopping at all stations, in order to accumulate technical data on acceleration. On a different occasion a K class Mogul

H1 class Brighton Atlantic Nº 2038 *Portland Bill* worked the first civilian 'Continental Express' to leave London since the withdrawal of Allied troops from France in 1940. Several years later, in the summer of 1947, Nº 2038 was based at Newhaven for the heavy boat trains, which had regained their pre-war popularity. It was a duty that it performed well and Nº 2038 *Portland Bill* is seen here at Eastleigh on 11 June 1949. (J. D. Darby - MLS)

was propelled to Three Bridges and back. After another visit to Brighton Works the SECR set was worked to Tunbridge Wells West and back without any trouble, but when Nº 239 worked its train to Hastings on 19 December 1948 it suffered a fractured right-hand valve rocker. After repairs and a series of more successful test runs, it made its first passenger trip on 14 March 1949 between Brighton and Redhill on the Hastings–Birkenhead through service. It then spent a period out of service before entering Brighton Works for the fitting of a spare boiler and some improvements to the valve gear. Repainted black and numbered 32039, the locomotive was freshly ex-works at the end of August 1949, the intention being that it would return to normal traffic, but in the event it saw no

further work, and in February 1951, following abandonment of the 'Leader' project, it was towed to Eastleigh Works for scrapping.

Following nationalisation the three surviving H1s — Nºs 2037 *Selsey Bill*, 2038 *Portland Bill* and 2039 *Hartland Point* — were given BR power rating '4P' and had 30,000 added to their numbers, while their

H1 class Brighton Atlantic Nº 2039 *Hartland Point* is seen here in Southern Railway days. In a previous existence, during LBSC days, it had been named *La France*. (J. D. Darby - MLS)

During July 1947, H1 class Atlantic Nº 32039 *Hartland Point*, previously named *La France* in LBSC days, was taken to Brighton Works for the fitting of sleeve valve gear, before being employed as a mobile experimental 'test-bed' for O. V. S. Bulleid's Leader class locomotive. Here is H1 class Atlantic Nº 32039 *Hartland Point* suitably modified for its test role, with Bulleid's Leader class 0-6-6-0T Nº 36001 on the left of the picture at Brighton, c.1949. *(J. D. Darby - (MLS))*

malachite-green livery gradually gave way to BR lined black, as by now they had been demoted to secondary passenger trains. Nº 32037 remained in unlined-black livery despite its boiler change in April 1949 at Brighton Works; Nº 32038 retained its malachite livery, while Nº 32039 was painted in unlined black during the valve-gear trials. Apart from these livery changes, a feature of the postwar years was the removal of the smokebox-fitted 'snifting' valves (automatic anti-vacuum valves used when coasting, 'snift' being the sound emitted).

Thereafter the surviving H1s all spent varying periods in store, occasionally at Eastbourne or Newhaven but more often at Brighton, finally being withdrawn during 1951 — all of them with more than a million miles to their credit. They were all broken up at Eastleigh Works, Nº 32037 *Selsey Bill* being dealt with on 6 September 1951.

Of the H1 class Atlantics, Nº 32037 *Selsey Bill* remained in unlined-black livery despite its boiler change in April 1949 at Brighton Works. Here we see number 37, on a train of LNWR carriage stock, c.1912. (John Scott-Morgan)

Here we see a work stained *Selsey Bill* at Bricklayers Arms depot on 10 June 1950. (John Scott-Morgan)

Chapter 10

THE H2 ATLANTICS

When ill health had forced D. E. Marsh to request a leave of absence his office was temporarily handed over to Lawson Billinton, then the District Locomotive Superintendent at New Cross Gate depot. When the Locomotive Committee met in March 1911 Billinton was instructed to work unlimited overtime at Brighton Works to ensure that the repair of as many as possible of the 150 locomotives and tenders waiting in the works for repair were successfully carried out to completion, in time for the approaching summer. The provision of building six new express passenger locomotives was considered, but was deferred until the April meeting. Marsh was not in attendance and in his absence the Locomotive Committee, together with Lawson Billinton agreed to play safe. On 4 April 1911 an order was placed for six superheated Atlantic locomotives to be constructed by Brighton Works. Numbered 421-6, they cost £3,265 each to construct and entered service between June 1911 and January 1912. Like their predecessors they were an 'instant success', but Marsh never got to know any of them, as his continuing 'ill health' forced him to tender his resignation on 19 July. Lawson Billinton continued in his acting capacity until 1 January 1912, when he was formally appointed

N° 421 was the first member of the six new 4-4-2 Atlantic class locomotives that were built for express passenger work between London and Brighton. The six locomotives were originally classified as H1/S class, meaning that the locomotives were like the H1 class, but with the addition of superheating. However, the group of six locomotives was soon adjusted to become H2 class, as although this second group of locomotives were very similar to the H1 class, they were different enough to warrant their own class heading, rather than become just a variant of the original H1 class Brighton Atlantics. Here we see N° 421, together with a fellow member of the H2 class, waiting to depart from Victoria Station with a heavily loaded passenger working. (Author)

A reverse view of H2 class Atlantic N° 422 showing detail of the tender livery markings. It is seen at Battersea shed with a round house roof visible at the smokebox end. (John Scott-Morgan)

When H2 class Atlantic N° 423 originally entered service, it was fitted with a speed indicator that cost £44. It retained its recorder until just before the Grouping in 1923. Here N° 423 is seen at London Bridge Station waiting to depart with a passenger service to Brighton. (Author)

Locomotive Superintendent, at a salary of £1,500 perannum.

The six new Atlantics were originally classified H1/S (H1 superheated), but this was amended to H2. The locomotives were very similar to the H1s and apart from the tube and smokebox alterations necessary for the addition of a Schmidt superheater, they differed from the earlier series by having larger cylinders, 10in piston valves, smokebox saddles, flared safety valve covers, Marsh built-up parallel chimneys, carriage heating equipment and the running plate was straightened between the cylinders and coupled wheels. However, because they were fitted with superheating equipment, the boiler pressure was reduced by 30lb to 170lb, as the intention was of reducing boiler maintenance costs and yet not affecting the

Here we see H2 class Atlantic N° 425 waiting to depart from Brighton with a fast passenger semi to London. The crisp and clean lines of the locomotive are there to be admired (John Scott-Morgan)

locomotives' performance. In SR days, when the earlier H1 class had been superheated, the boiler pressure of these locomotives was increased to 200lb, so this pressure became standard for both classes.

The LBSCR probably made greater use of speed-recorders on its locomotives than did any other pre-Grouping railway, although there was a period following the removal of Stroudley's patent device during which drivers had to employ their own judgement. During 1909 Hasler speed-recorders were fitted to H1s N°s 39-41 (as indeed they would be to other main-line locomotives built in later years and retrospectively to some earlier locomotives). The speed-recorder worked by means

of a crank connected to the big-end on the right-hand side of the locomotive, the movement of which was transmitted through reduction gearing to a perforator which punctured an appropriate record of the speed on a continuously moving roll of squared paper located within a holder attached to the inside of the cab. When N°s 421-6 entered service they were also fitted with speed indicators, which cost £44 each. N°s 421-4 retained their recorders until just before the Grouping, N° 421 being the last to have this equipment removed, in September 1925.

Located between the frames and ahead of the saddle casting was the Westinghouse pump.

The superheater was fitted with dampers operated by means of small steam cylinders on the smokebox sides, but they were found to be unnecessary and were later removed. As was the case with the H1 class, auxiliary guard-irons were attached ahead of the bogie frames, and the bogie wheels were braked, although (again as with the H1s) these brakes would later be removed.

N° 421 entered traffic painted in slate-grey primer, albeit fully lined out in black and white, and did not receive its full umber livery until June 1913. N°s 422/4/6 entered service in unlined grey, running thus for a few weeks, while N° 423 completed its 1,000 miles of

Work on building two spare boilers commenced at Brighton Works in March 1913. They were stored unfinished until October 1915, when one was completed and fitted to N° 421. It was generally similar to those carried when new, apart from modified tube arrangements. Here is a model of N° 421 in umber livery, currently on display at The Brighton Toy & Model Museum. (Author) (Courtesy of The Brighton Toy & Model Museum, Brighton)

running-in with just a coat of red oxide for embellishment.

When N° 421 left the erecting shop at Brighton it had a short cab roof, but before it posed for the official photographer and entered service a rearward section was added giving the footplate crew added protection. The rest of the class were similarly altered when built. N°s 421 and 422 also differed in having a thicker and less sharply curved valance at the leading end, but whereas N° 421 was altered to conform with the final four locomotives N° 422 was left to soldier on for some years before being similarly modified.

Of the new H2 locomotives introduced between June 1911 and January 1912 Brighton shed received N°s 421 and 425, Battersea N°s 422 and 426, and Eastbourne N°s 423 and 424. They shared with the 'H1s' the express passenger services between London and Brighton, which included the heavily loaded 'Brighton Limited' and 'Southern Belle' Pullman trains — described by the LBSCR as the most luxurious in the world. The H2s were an immediate success

with crews; their performance was good, and their coal consumption was around 10-12½ per cent lower than that of the saturated H1s when working similar duties. Lawson Billinton explained in May 1912 that most H2 drivers employed relatively long cut-off (the point during the piston stroke at which the inlet valve is closed) and partly closed the regulators, whereas with the H1s it was general practice to leave the regulator wide open and adjusted the speed by altering the cut-off. The superheated H2s gave little cause for concern and worked respectable mileages during the 1915 period. So successful was the fitting of superheaters that, in later years, the Southern Railway superheated the H1s, although it has been said that, even in their original (saturated) form, these earlier locomotives performed better than did the H2s.

Work was started on building two spare boilers at Brighton Works in March 1913, but they remained unfinished and were stored until October 1915, when one was finally completed and was fitted to N° 421. It was a similar boiler to those

that were carried when new, apart from modified tube arrangements. The other boiler was sold to the Government in January 1916 and was despatched to Vickers for conversion as a stationary boiler for use at the Royal Navy mine depot at Grangemouth. The boiler which was now left as the spare was provided with 143 2¼in steel tubes, and in November 1915 it was fitted to N° 426. When re-tubing of the class's boilers became necessary the number of small tubes became the standard layout until 1926 for the six original boilers.

In 1912 the B4 4-4-0s found themselves largely relegated to the LBSCR's secondary and coastal services, and until the Grouping in 1923 main-line duties were generally shared by the 11 Atlantic tender engines, the J1 and J2 4-6-2Ts and the L-class 4-6-4Ts, although some assistance was provided by the I3 4-4-2 tanks. Early in 1917 H2s N°s 422 and 426 were transferred to Brighton, joining N°s 421 and 425, but N°s 423 and 424 remained at Eastbourne.

Following the Grouping all of the Atlantic tender engines were repainted in Maunsell dark-green livery as they went through the works, although the umber livery of N°s 39, 423 and 425 lasted so well that they were not so treated until 1926/7. N° 423 ran for a time with Southern number-plates attached to the cab sides, with its number on the buffer-beam and 'LBSC' lettering on the tender sides, but on its next works visit numbers were added to the tender. At about this time N° 38 was running with number-plates, no cab-side numerals and blank tender sides.

In 1925 the Southern Railway's Publicity Department, based at Waterloo, decided that the company's image needed to be improved and decreed that express passenger locomotives should be named. This move it thought would generate an interest with travellers and would provide an inexpensive source of advertising focusing on various South Coast landmarks. Thus during the next few years, all new passenger locomotives, as well as existing express passenger locomotives, were named. On the Central Section this included the H1 and H2 Atlantics. The nameplates, which were curved to fit the driving-wheel splashers, were cast in brass with raised lettering and they were given red backgrounds.

Between being painted in Southern Railway green in September 1924 and with being named *South Foreland* in February 1926 N° 421 was involved in a strange accident on 14 November 1925. Passing Haywards Heath with the 9.40am West Worthing–London express, it suffered a catastrophic failure of its rear coupled axle. Fortunately there

was no derailment, and no one was injured, but delays to traffic were very severe.

N° 426 was fitted with vacuum ejectors, but the other members of the H2 class were fitted with the Westinghouse system. Just after the Grouping, after Eastleigh Works had assumed responsibility for the H1s and H2s, the Westinghouse hoses were removed and, in several cases, the pipes blanked off, although the wheels remained air-braked.

Between April and June 1929 the footsteps of H2s were inset to fit in with the more restricted Eastern Section loading gauge, and between 1935 and 1937 other alterations were made to reduce the overall height and width: The Marsh chimney was replaced by the parallel cast-iron Ashford U1 pattern; the dome cover was lowered by 45/16in; the safety-valve levers were shortened; the eaves of the cab were rounded off, the buffer-beam ends were shaved off and the whistle was attached to the safety valve casing. At this same time, advantage was taken to fit Drummond whistles, standard SR-pattern lamp brackets and tube-cleaning apparatus. The tube cleaning apparatus connection was sited on the left-hand top slope of the smokebox and consisted of a screwed connection, to which tube blowing lances could be secured by means of flexible piping, in order to scour the tubes by high pressure steam when on shed.

Also fitted was de-greasing apparatus, whereby a diagonal pipe, fitted between the driving and trailing wheels, delivered hot water to the rail head to clean it of grease and sand and thus maintain good

electrical conductivity for the track circuitry. It was also standard at this time to line the tender coal-rails with sheet steel plating to prevent the loss of small coal when it was stacked high.

The various mechanical issues having been resolved after the years immediately following the Grouping, the Atlantics settled down to their routine duties. However, when the new 'King Arthurs' and 'Rivers' reached Central Section sheds in 1925/6 they suffered a noticeable decline in status, a number being transferred to Eastbourne and Bognor Regis, those at the latter shed now reaching London by way of the difficult mid-Sussex route or along the coast line to Hove and thence via the Cliftonville Spur.

Waterloo also imposed restrictions as to the services that could be worked by Atlantics, to ensure that the loads that they worked were readily manageable. Thus when SR corridor stock was introduced in January 1930 the 3.30pm Victoria–Bognor Regis, which ran via the mid-Sussex line and which was formed regularly of seven coaches and two Pullman cars, was deemed to be 'outside the Atlantics' capacity'. To rectify the problem it was decided to provide a pilot locomotive as far as Horsham. After a month or so the loading was reduced, removing the need for a pilot locomotive, and thereafter the Atlantic went unassisted; then, with the introduction of the summer service, the load was increased again, although no more was heard of piloting. It was also decreed that the maximum un-piloted load for the Victoria–Newhaven

'Continentals' should be 10 coaches, but this too underestimated the Atlantics' capabilities, for prewar boat trains had regularly loaded up to 480 tons tare.

Ahead of electrification in 1933 LSWR-designed 'King Arthur' 4-6-0s with six-wheel tenders took over much of the passenger work on the Brighton main line. Electrification of the latter took away much of the Atlantics' remaining work, although they still managed to make themselves useful. At this time N°s 2421/2, along with H1s N°s 2037-41, were allocated to Eastbourne and 2423-6 to Bognor Regis. The last four remained at Bognor, where they were maintained in

fine condition, both mechanically and externally and they worked all of the principal turns to London until July 1938, but the locomotives allocated to Eastbourne did not stay there very long, N°s 2038 and 2039 moving to Newhaven for boat-train workings, while the other five were displaced from February 1933 by 'Schools' 4-4-0s N°s 910 *Merchant Taylors*, 911 *Dover*, 912 *Downside*, 913 *Christ's Hospital*, 914 *Eastbourne*, 915 *Brighton* and 916 *Whitgift*; in the summer those still remaining were transferred to New Cross. The H2s were to be found on the secondary routes from London to Brighton via Shoreham (approximately 2½ hours), via Uckfield and via the

Bluebell line (approximately three hours, but with a scheduled stop at East Grinstead).

In LBSCR days both classes of Atlantic tender engine had been allowed over the Heathfield line, and following the opening of the Ashurst Junction route in 1914 Eastbourne-allocated N°s 423 and 424 were noted working on this route with through London services. After the Grouping, however, the Southern barred them from the 'Cuckoo Line' between Polegate and Eridge, and the embargo was never lifted, although N° 2421 *South Foreland* was noted on 17 June 1951 working local services between Hailsham and Eastbourne.

In January 1938, H2 class N° 2423 *The Needles* gave excellent results on the 12:35 Victoria - Ramsgate service and the 20:13 return, working with loads of 230 tons. The conclusion of these trials was that N° 2421, N° 2423, N° 2425 and N° 2426 were made available to the Eastern Section in time for the summer services. They were maintained at Battersea shed, with fitters long-familiar with the class and crewed by men familiar with 4-4-2 wheel arrangements on express workings. They gave good service '... as long as they weren't overloaded'. N° 2425 *Trevose Head* is seen at Newhaven in June 1949. (W. Boot)

In January 1938 H1 N° 2041 *Peveril Point* was chosen for a series of trials over the Chatham line, but it did not steam well and was exchanged for H2 N° 2423 *The Needles*, which did gave excellent results, particularly on the 12.35pm Victoria–Ramsgate service and the 8.13pm return working, with loads of 230 tons. It was concluded that N°s 2421/3/5/6 should be made available to the Eastern Section in time for the summer services. The locomotives were sent to Battersea shed, which had fitters long familiar with the class and crews familiar with the 4-4-2 wheel arrangement on express workings. The use of the H2s on the Eastern Section was a success, providing that the locomotives were not overloaded. However, from the summer of 1939, when electrification was extended to the Medway Towns, there was no longer a shortage of passenger locomotives, and thereafter the H2s were restricted to the Central Section.

On the Central Section H1 N° 2039 *Hartland Point* and H2 N° 2424 *Beachy Head* resumed work on the Newhaven boat trains, although they were often piloted by an ancient ex-SECR B1 or F1 4-4-0. Boat-train traffic increased to such a level that it was common for 13 coaches and three or four vans to be the norm, for those wishing to travel abroad via this service. Boiler pressure of all Atlantics was standardised at 200lb, which also helped with the exchanging of boilers at overhaul.

The livery changes mandated by O. V. S. Bulleid began to take effect in February 1939, when H1 N° 2040 *St Catherine's Point* emerged from Eastleigh displaying the new-style lettering and numerals (the numbers now back on the cab sides rather than the tender), and the rest of the class were similarly treated over the next few years. German victories in France during May 1940 brought about an abrupt curtailment of the boat-train services, with the result

that the Atlantics now had even fewer chances to perform what they were designed to do, and a number were placed in store.

In November 1940 the H2s were transferred to Basingstoke, displacing six Class N15X 'Remembrance' 4-6-0s (Maunsell rebuilds of L. B. Billinton's Baltic tanks), which in turn were sent on loan to the GWR. In due course the 'H2s' moved on again, reaching as far as Salisbury, Eastleigh and Southampton. Indeed on 11 March 1941 N° 2422 *North Foreland* was recorded at Bournemouth working a troop train, while on 17 July 1941 N° 2421 *South Foreland* was noted at Dorchester on a vans working.

From February 1941 plain black became the standard colour for all locomotives, remaining thus until the end of the war, but it was October 1942 before the first two Atlantics, H1 N° 2039 *Hartland Point* and H2 N° 2424 *Beachy Head*, succumbed to this livery.

By January 1943 the 'Schools' 4-4-0s allocated to Bournemouth depot were experiencing operating difficulties, as their tenders had insufficient water for heavy wartime trains and were losing time by taking water stops *en route*. 'Lord Nelson' 4-6-0s were therefore sent to replace the 'Schools', which went to Basingstoke, in turn displacing Atlantics N°s 2421-6 to Ashford. As a direct result of this reshuffle the 1.15pm from Charing Cross to Dover was worked regularly by an Atlantic instead of an ex-SECR L-class 4-4-0. Also of interest was the 12.25pm from Charing Cross, which was shared with N° 1275, a superheated E-class 4-4-0. Various other local duties were also worked, including those to Tonbridge, Margate, Ramsgate and Maidstone East. At Ashford they replaced five L-class 4-4-0s, of which N°s 1775-8 moved on to Faversham and No 1779 to Ramsgate. But the L-class locomotives were badly missed by their crews for their ability at hard slogging, despite the fact that the H2s were better at acceleration and faster on level track. Compared with the Atlantics, the 4-4-0s were considered to be better at pick-up goods and yard shunting, which comes as no surprise, for the Atlantics were designed as express passenger locomotives rather than mixed-traffic types.

Thus in February 1944 it seemed that all were happy to see the Atlantics return to their spiritual home of Brighton, joining elder sisters N°s 2037 *Selsey Bill*, 2038 *Portland Bill* and 2039 *Hartland Point*. The 'H1s' had recently been transferred to Brighton from New Cross Gate, where they had spent the war years. N° 2040 *St Catherine's Point* and N° 2041 *Peveril Point* were condemned in January and March 1944, with mileages of 999,944 and 1,000,080 miles respectively. N° 2041 was broken up at Eastleigh in March 1944, while N° 2040 was left forgotten in the scrap line for many years, until it was moved away to Kimbridge Junction on 15 January 1948. Later it was moved to Romsey and was finally cut up at the former RAF depot at Dinton in July 1948.

The works at Brighton and Eastleigh were struggling to deal with the large backlog of Western and Central Section locomotives awaiting repair, and as a consequence Atlantics Nos 2037 *Selsey Bill*, 2038 *Portland Bill*, 2422

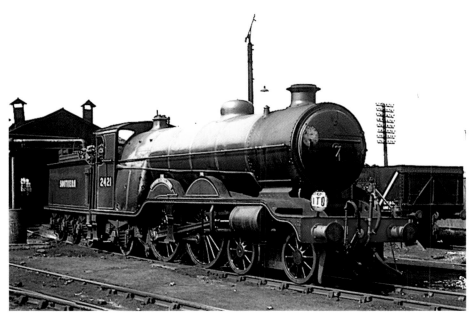

North Foreland, 2424 *Beachy Head* and 2426 *St Alban's Head* all received general or intermediate overhauls at Ashford; the intention was to paint all of the Atlantics in malachite green as circumstances permitted, but they were turned out in unlined black. The H2s were nevertheless all in green by October 1947, but of the H1s only N° 2038 *Portland Bill* was treated; N° 2039 *Hartland Point* became a test locomotive for O. V. S. Bulleid's 'Leader' class, while N° 2037 *Selsey Bill* was not considered worth a general repair after leaving Ashford Works in September 1945, although it did have a change of boiler in April 1949, without the benefit of a fresh coat of paint. N°s 2040 *St Catherine's Point* and 2041 *Peveril Point* had, of course, long since been condemned.

Normal working of the 'Continental Express' boat-train service had resumed in 1945, even before the end of hostilities, and by the summer of 1947 H2s N°s 2422 *North Foreland*, 2423 *The Needles* and

2426 *St Alban's Head* (plus H1 N° 2038) were based at Newhaven for working these heavy trains. At this time Brighton-allocated N° 2421 *South Foreland* was used regularly on the 8.18am Uckfield–Victoria and 6.10pm return (a duty it shared with 'H1s' Nos 2037 and 2039), while N°s 2424 *Beachy Head* and 2425 *Trevose Head*, based at New Cross, shared workings on the 3.25am London Bridge–Brighton passenger and van train, returning with the 6.58am Brighton–Uckfield–London Bridge. On 16 July 1947 the boat-train platforms at Newhaven Harbour station were opened for electric traction, and with effect from 15 May 1949 the principal boat-train duties were handed over to the Bulleid/Raworth-designed Co-Co electric locomotives N°s 20001 (built in 1941), 20002 (1945) and 20003 (1948). However, the majority of relief boat trains at busy periods continued to be worked by Atlantics.

Following the nationalisation

N° **32424** is seen again wearing SR livery but this time at Stewarts Lane depot in August 1949. (MLS)

From 15 May 1949, the principal Newhaven boat train duties were handed over to the Bulleid/Raworth designed Co-Co electric locomotives: N° 20001 (built in 1941 and originally numbered CC1) and N° 20002 (built in 1945 and originally numbered CC2). Both locomotives were built at Ashford. A third locomotive, N° 20003, had been built at Brighton in 1948. However, the Brighton Atlantics continued to work the majority of relief boat trains at busy periods. Here is the first of the group seen as originally numbered (CC1) working in sidings with its overhead collector up. (Ernie Pay)

of Britain's railways the H2s were renumbered by the addition of 30,000 to their existing numbers and, having by now been relegated to secondary passenger duties, gradually forsook SR malachite green for BR lined black. N° 32421 *South Foreland* was repainted thus at Eastleigh Works in May 1949 and again in the same livery at Eastleigh in November 1951 and at Brighton in October 1954. N° 32422 *North Foreland* was repainted in lined black at Brighton in March 1951. N° 32424 *Beachy Head* passed through an intermediate stage with BR numerals and smokebox-door numberplate but retaining its green livery; it was repainted in lined black at Eastleigh in September 1951 and again at Eastleigh in March 1954. N° 32425 *Trevose Head* gained lined black at Eastleigh in October 1950, N° 32426 *St Alban's Head* being treated similarly at Brighton in August 1955. The odd one out was *The Needles*, which at the beginning of 1948 was at Eastleigh Works for a boiler change and returned to service in early January as N° 2423, before use of the temporary S number prefix had been authorised; still in malachite green and bearing its pre-nationalisation number, it was withdrawn in May 1949 with badly cracked frames and worn cylinders, having covered 905,146 miles.

In BR days a number of workings became synonymous with the H2s, most notably the heavy rush-hour trains that ran between Victoria and East Grinstead and the Brighton–Plymouth services, which they were booked to work as far as Portsmouth, although there was a report of one as far west as Yeovil Junction. On summer Saturdays they were also tasked with hauling heavy inter-regional trains consisting of carmine-and-cream Stanier-designed coaches, which they would work as far as Kensington Olympia or Mitre Bridge Junction.

Following nationalisation all of the remaining ex-LBSCR Atlantic

Bulleid/Raworth designed Co-Co electric locomotive, originally numbered CC1, was built in 1941 and renumbered as N° 20001 at nationalisation. It was built at Ashford along with CC2 (N° 20002), unlike the third member of the class which was built at Brighton. (John Scott-Morgan)

Although a third locomotive, N° 20003, had been constructed at Brighton during 1948, the Brighton Atlantics continued to work the majority of the relief Newhaven boat trains at busy periods. Here is the third Bulleid/Raworth designed Co-Co electric locomotive to be built. (John Scott-Morgan)

tender engines spent periods in store, occasionally at Eastbourne or Newhaven but more often at Brighton, and it was widely anticipated that they would all be withdrawn in 1951, but as it turned out only the three surviving H1s succumbed that year. The H2s were granted a stay of execution, and over the next few years they proved to be excellent replacements for the 2-6-4Ts, Pacifics and other younger locomotives on the through Brighton–Bournemouth/Plymouth services; they were also in particular demand at Christmastime for working parcels specials between London Bridge or Bricklayers Arms to Brighton, Eastbourne and Hastings. Their time in store apparently had little or no effect on their performance or reliability when they were fired up again.

H2 Atlantic Nº 2424 *BeachyHead* was based at New Cross and shared workings on the 3.25am London Bridge–Brighton passenger and van train, returning with the 6.58am Brighton–Uckfield–London Bridge. It is seen here in SR livery at New Cross depot with B4X Nº 2056 on 21 May 1948. (MLS)

Nº 32424, an H2 class Atlantic, is seen in light steam wearing SR livery, but with a BR number at Battersea depot on 12 August 1949. (MLS)

Indeed, between 29 September 1952 and 15 November 1952 Nº 32421 *South Foreland* was noted on 34 of a possible 48 Brighton–Bournemouth workings, four of those missed being taken by Nº 32426.

When the Railway Correspondence & Travel Society ran the two Brighton Works Centenary specials, on 5 and 19 October 1952, it offered all-Pullman accommodation at fast speeds to intending participants. Nº 32424

Beachy Head worked the first trip, with a Newhaven crew, while Nº 32425 *Trevose Head* worked the second, with a Brighton crew. Both excursions were timed to match the one-hour journey time of the steam-hauled 'Southern Belle' and managed creditable timings. The route for both trips was Victoria–Battersea Park–Pouparts Junction–Clapham Junction–Balham–Streatham Common–Norbury–Selhurst–Windmill Bridge Junction–

East Croydon–Purley–Coulsdon North–Three Bridges–Brighton. On the down run on 5 October No 32424 suffered a permanent-way check in the East Croydon area which caused a loss of time between Windmill Bridge and Coulsdon North, but this was later made up. Indeed, the locomotive was running slightly hot by the end of the down run and needed attention before returning in the evening on the up working, which reached 80mph

Another H2 class Atlantic was seen in shed on 28 August 1949, this time at Newhaven. Although the railways had been nationalised for some 20 months, it is still sporting its Southern number of Nº 2425. (MLS)

N° **32422** *North Foreland* was repainted in BR lined black livery at Brighton Works in March 1951 and is seen here at Brighton depot in this form. (T. Owen)

N° **32421** *South Foreland* was noted working thirty-four out of the forty-eight possible Brighton - Bournemouth services between 29 September 1952 and 15 November 1952. N° 32421 *South Foreland* is seen at Fratton in May 1953 in a work-stained manner. (J. Davenport)

near Horley but was checked in the London area, although it did arrive on time. The load on both days was eight Pullman vehicles, a total of 319 tons tare, 340 tons full.

On 3 May 1953 the Stephenson Locomotive Society ran its London–Portsmouth 'SLS Special'. N° 32425 *Trevose Head* worked this train from Victoria via Balham Junction,

Crystal Palace, Norwood Junction, West Croydon, Sutton, Leatherhead, Dorking North, Horsham (where it took water), Pulborough, Barnham, Chichester, Havant and Fratton to Portsmouth & Southsea. The return journey — to Waterloo — was worked by Drummond-designed Class T9 'Greyhound' 4-4-0 N° 30718, dating from 1899.

N° 32424 *Beachy Head* continued to make occasional appearances on relief Newhaven boat trains. On 22 May 1954 it worked the 5.48pm up service, loaded to 435 tons, and although seven minutes were lost to signal and permanent-way restrictions the deficit had been recovered by the time the train reached Victoria.

Atlantics worked two more rail-tours during 1955, the first of these being the 'Hampshireman' on 6 February, N° 32421 *South Foreland* being used for the first leg, from Waterloo via Clapham Junction, Hounslow, Staines Central, Chertsey and Woking as far as Guildford, before returning light-engine direct to the Brighton line at Redhill — probably the first time this ex-SECR cross-country route had seen such a locomotive. The excursion then continued with 'E5X' 0-6-2Ts N°s 32570 and 32576 from Guildford to Horsham and thence to Petersfield, from where 'Greyhound' 4-4-0s N°s 30301 and 30732 worked 'the last train to run the complete length of the Meon Valley Railway' (which closed to passenger traffic the following day) back to Waterloo.

The second excursion in 1955, postponed from 12 June due to an ASLEF strike, was the 'Wealden Limited' of 14 August. This train,

The **RCTS** ran two 'Brighton Works Centenary Specials' on 5 and 19 October 1952. The first was worked by N° 32424 *Beachy Head* with a Newhaven crew. Both excursions were timed to complete the one hour journey of the old steam-hauled '*Southern Belle*' service and managed to achieve respectable timings. During the run on 5 October, N° 32424 *Beachy Head* had a permanent way check in the East Croydon area in the down direction, which caused a loss of time between Windmill Bridge and Coulsdon North, but this was later made up. The up-train reached 80mph near Horley, but was checked in the London area. N° 32424 *Beachy Head* was running slightly hot at the end of the down run and needed attention before the return run in the evening. The load was 8 Pullman vehicles at 319 tare, 340 tons full. N° 32424 *Beachy Head* is seen with this very special on Grosvenor Bank, having just left Victoria on 5 October 1952. (MLS)

N° 32424 *Beachy Head* is seen at Brighton on 5 October 1952 waiting to depart with the return RCTS working to Victoria, where it reached 80 mph near Horley. (T. Owen)

Nº **32425** *Trevose Head* is seen taking water at Horsham in May 1953 before continuing on to Portsmouth & Southsea with the Stephenson Locomotive Society's special train from Victoria to Portsmouth. (J. Davenport)

'*The Wealden Limited*' ran on 14 August 1955 and worked its way from Victoria to Lewis by a variety of locomotives, before H2 class Atlantic Nº 32426 *St Albans Head* took over the train and worked over the closed 'Bluebell' line to New Cross Gate. Nº 32426 *St Albans Head* is seen waiting to depart from Lewes during this tour, shortly before it travelled over the closed Bluebell Railway. (E. V. Fry)

which included a Pullman buffet car, worked its way from Victoria via Nunhead, Lewisham, New Beckenham, Beckenham Junction, Swanley, Otford, Sevenoaks, Tonbridge, Hawkhurst, Hastings and Lewes, where Nº 32426 *St Alban's Head* took over for a run to Brighton and back, the train then travelling via Sheffield Park, Horsted Keynes, East Grinstead and East Croydon to New Cross Gate, where 'E6X' 0-6-2T Nº 32411 replaced the Atlantic for the final leg back to Victoria via Peckham Rye and Battersea Park.

In May 1956 the five remaining H2s were suddenly taken out of service for inspection of their bogie frames. This was as a direct result of an inquiry into a derailment on the Eastern Region on 1 September 1955, when the 3.50pm express from King's Cross to Leeds became completely derailed a few yards beyond the facing points of Westwood Junction. The service was being worked by the unique ex-LNER Class W1 4-6-4, Nº 60700, and the cause of the derailment was found to be a complete fracture of the right-hand frame plate of the locomotive's bogie. Inspection of the H2s (which, being of broadly Doncaster design, had bogie framing similar to that of Nº 60700) revealed flaws on Nºs 32421 *South Foreland* and 32426 *St Alban's Head*, which as a result were set aside until officially condemned in August 1956. Meanwhile Nº 32422 *North Foreland* was restricted to light duties, being used thus until it failed with a broken left-hand cylinder just as it was about to work a ramblers' special from East Croydon to Marlow, Nº 32425 *Trevose Head* being substituted.

Kept busy almost to the end on the Brighton–Bournemouth service and the Hastings–Manchester through service as far as Willesden, Nº 32425 bade a final farewell to the boat-train services on 5 August 1956, when it worked the 6.23am Newhaven–Victoria, the 10.25am Victoria–Newhaven and the 5.41pm

back to Victoria, where a 1½min-early arrival was booked. By now its days were numbered due to badly cracked frames and worn cylinders, and, along with Nº 32422, it was condemned in October 1956. Following withdrawal it was used to provide steam to heat the EMU depot at Slade Green (from December 1956 until April 1957) while the coal-powered heating plant was being converted to oil; for this purpose its boiler was adjusted to give a maximum working pressure of 100lb. Meanwhile other members of the class were called in turn to Brighton Works for scrapping, Nº 32421 *South Foreland*, in November 1956, being followed by Nºs 32422 *North Foreland* and 32426 *St Alban's Head* in March 1957.

Nº 32424 *Beachy Head* survived a brief visit to Eastleigh Works in August 1956 and spent much of its time thereafter on the through Bournemouth service. On 17 January 1957 the locomotive developed a hot axle-box at Fareham, and, having returned to Brighton at the end of the month, it was left out in the open. However, it had been booked to work the Locomotive Club of Great Britain 'Southern Counties Limited' rail-tour on 24 February, so after some hasty repairs it was sent out on a trial run, and, having successfully worked the 11.18pm vans to London Bridge and returned with the following day's 5.32am fish train, it was declared fit to work the LCGB railtour.

Brighton H2 class Atlantic Nº 32421 *South Foreland* is seen in BR lined livery at Redhill, on 28 July 1951. (N. Harrop – MLS)

Brighton H2 class Atlantic Nº 32421 *South Foreland* is seen working a Brighton - Plymouth train as it departs Southampton Central on 3 August 1953. (N. Harrop – MLS)

After its withdrawal in September 1956, H2 class 4-4-2 Atlantic Nº 32425 *Trevose Head* had its boiler pressure reduced to 100psi. It was then sent to Slade Green EMU depot in Kent for use as a temporary stationary boiler, while the depot's heating plant was being converted from coal to oil-firing. It was there from January to April 1957. (W. M. J. Jackson)

The special started (in atrocious weather) from Marylebone, GNR-built 'N5/2' 0-6-2 tank engines Nᵒˢ 69257 and 69319 working the train to Kew East Junction via Wembley Stadium. Nᵒ 32424, which had been sent to Kew Bridge, now took over, the train heading towards Brighton by way of Clapham Junction, Factory Junction, Nunhead, Lewisham, Sanderstead and East Grinstead. However, as it drew into the platform at Horsted Keynes the locomotive, suffering from an overheated big-end, was seen to be badly leaking steam and was consequently replaced by 'C2X' 0-6-0 Nᵒ 32437, which took the train onward via Sheffield Park and Lewes to Brighton and thence

to Preston Park. From here the train was worked by Nᵒ 80152 as far as Havant, where the BR Standard tank was replaced by ex-LBSCR 'Terrier' 0-6-0Ts Nᵒˢ 32636 and 32650 for a run to Hayling Island and back. Nᵒ 80152 then took the train on from Havant to Portsmouth Harbour, from where 'Schools' 4-4-0 Nᵒ 30929 *Malvern* worked the tour's final leg to Waterloo via Guildford.

Following its exertions on 24 February *Beachy Head* was laid aside at Brighton, its duties being taken over by ex-SECR L-class 4-4-0s Nᵒˢ 31776 and 31777. When steamed again, on 18 June, it emulated Nᵒ 32422 by blowing out the front cover plate of the left-hand cylinder, but luckily a spare

plate was to hand from Nᵒ 32425 *Trevose Head*, which had been towed back from Slade Green. Repairs were completed by 22 July, and on the 23rd Nᵒ 32424 was successfully employed on the 11.18pm vans to London Bridge and the following day's 5.32am down fish train. Nᵒ 32425, the penultimate Brighton Atlantic, finally succumbed to the scrapman in August.

During its final year of existence *Beachy Head* accumulated a decent mileage on a wide variety of duties, also making a guest appearance at the Eastleigh Works open day on 7 August 1957, the preparation for which included some vigorous cleaning that reportedly revealed traces of umber! Two days later

The last of the Atlantics to survive was H2 class Nᵒ 32424 *Beachy Head*, whose swan song was an enthusiasts' special '*The Sussex Coast Limited*', on 13 April 1958, over the route it had made its own: Victoria to Newhaven. It is seen here at Victoria just before departure. (MLS)

H2 class Nº 32424 *Beachy Head* worked an enthusiasts' special '*The Sussex Coast Limited*' on 13 April 1958 from Victoria to Newhaven. It is seen here at Newhaven after the run from Victoria. (MLS)

it was back at Brighton, working a Brighton–Sheffield empty-stock train as far as Willesden. On 17 August it worked a Brighton–Manchester relief but had to be retired to Stewarts Lane for superheater repairs. During October

it was used on five occasions, working the Bournemouth through train, and during November and December it worked a further 17 trips. Its penultimate run of 1957 came on 21 December, when, running in a very dirty

condition, it was noted heading south through Purley Oaks with a train of 30-odd vans, and the following day it worked the 2.31pm vans from Brighton to Bricklayers Arms, returning at 9.50pm. But by Christmas Eve it was out of use at Brighton, awaiting a final run on behalf of the Railway Correspondence & Travel Society.

Now the last surviving Atlantic, Nº 32424 *Beachy Head* would perform its swansong on an enthusiasts' special, the RCTS 'Sussex Coast Limited', over the Victoria–Newhaven route on 13 April 1958, an in preparation for this run the locomotive was cleaned and steamed on 9 April and, after a run on a London Bridge vans working, declared fit for duty. The special consisted of seven corridor coaches, including Pullman car *Myrtle*, giving a total train load of 255 tons, and despite two signal stops, two signal checks and a 15mph permanent-way slack Nº 32424 covered the 56.8 miles from Victoria to Newhaven in 81min 11sec, the net time being calculated as 70min, against a scheduled time of 80min (surely as gallant an end as that of GNR Atlantic Nº 62822, which on a foggy 26 November 1950 had hauled the 'Ivatt Atlantic Special' 156 miles from King's Cross to Doncaster exactly to schedule in 3 hours 15 minutes). 'Terrier' 0-6-0 Nº 32640, which as LBSCR Nº 40 *Brighton* had won a gold medal at Paris in 1878, worked the train between Newhaven Harbour and Newhaven Town, and from there Standard tank Nº 80154 — the last steam locomotive to be built at Brighton — worked the train to Lewes and

After working the enthusiasts' special to Brighton Nº 32424 *Beachy Head* then moved to Brighton loco shed for the very last time. Here it is seen backing out of Brighton Station with Brighton Works in the background. (P. Hughes)

Brighton, whence 'King Arthur' Nº 30796 *Sir Dodinas Le Savage* took it back to Victoria.

After working the special Nº 32424 retired to Brighton shed for the very last time. It made its final journey to Eastleigh on 24 April 1958, not merely under its own steam but hauling the 7.28am Lancing–Micheldever, comprising a 12-car rake of empty coaching stock. Dismantling of the locomotive began on 18 May and according to official records was completed on 31 May. Subsequently one of its *Beachy Head* nameplates was presented to the Mayor of Eastbourne. It is noteworthy that this locomotive was not only the last of the Brighton Atlantics to survive; it was also the last express passenger locomotive of the 4-4-2 wheel arrangement to work for British Railways, having outlasted the ex-GNR Ivatt Atlantics.

Not long after its withdrawal in 1958 and looking in immaculate condition, H2 class 4-4-2 locomotive Nº 32424 *Beachy Head* is seen at Eastleigh Works. It was the very last Atlantic express passenger locomotive to run a normal passenger service in this country. Sadly, it was dismantled in just two weeks and became no more than a memory. (Author)

The actual death throes of the former LBSCR's H2 class 4-4-2 Atlantic Nº 32424 *Beachy Head* began at Eastleigh Works on 18 May 1958. Two weeks later the scrapping process was completed and Nº 32424 *Beachy Head* officially ceased to exist. In this view we can see the exposed hard wood blocks that were used as an effective form of insulation around the boiler. (Ron Fisher)

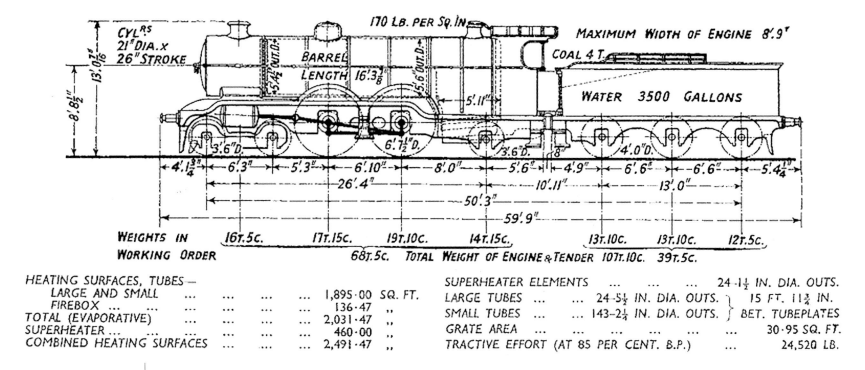

HEATING SURFACES, TUBES—

LARGE AND SMALL	...	...	...	...	1,895·00 SQ. FT.
FIREBOX	...	...	...	...	136·47 ,,
TOTAL (EVAPORATIVE)	...	...	...	...	2,031·47 ,,
SUPERHEATER ...	...	...	...	...	460·00 ,,
COMBINED HEATING SURFACES	...	...	...	2,491·47 ,,

SUPERHEATER ELEMENTS ... ... 24 -1¼ IN. DIA. OUTS.

LARGE TUBES ... ... 24-5½ IN. DIA. OUTS. ⎫ 15 FT. 11¾ IN.

SMALL TUBES ... ... 143-2¼ IN. DIA. OUTS. ⎬ BET. TUBEPLATES

GRATE AREA ... ... 30·95 SQ. FT.

TRACTIVE EFFORT (AT 85 PER CENT. B.P.) ... 24,520 LB.

An official diagram showing the leading dimensions of the Brighton Line H2 class Atlantic locomotives.
(Author)

Chapter 11

THE ATLANTIC TANKS

The I1s

Constructed in 1906/7, the LBSCR's first Atlantic tank engines were the I1s, designed by D. E. Marsh for suburban work. Twenty were built, in two batches, the first 10 being numbered 595-604, the remainder 1-10. The second batch used the coupled wheels and motion from recently scrapped Stroudley D1s

and D2s, the wheelbase being consequently reduced from 8ft 9in to 7ft 7in.

The class pioneer N° 595, emerged from Brighton Works in September 1906, its design being based largely on that of H. A. Ivatt's C12 4-4-2 tanks of 1898. Along with sister locomotive N° 596 it had a straight-sided smokebox, a tapered

boiler and a rooftop clerestory, which had adjustable venting louvres. Crews had complained about ventilation in the cab, particularly as the water tank sides encroached into the cab space. That the I1 design was not a success was due mainly to its very small boiler, which was unable to provide the steam needed to do the job.

N° 598 was part of the batch of the first ten I1 class 4-4-2 tank Atlantics designed by D. E. Marsh. The batch were numbered N° 595 - N° 604 and incorporated the wheels, coupling-rods and parts of the motion from older D1 and D2 class engines, which had previously been taken out of service. (Author)

Brighton Atlantic tank N° 1 , with its magic number, was ironically one of the last members of the I1 class to be constructed. Its first Southern Railway number was B1, later becoming 2001. In BR days it was given the number 32001, before being finally withdrawn from service at Brighton in July 1948, and scrapped in November that same year. (John Scott-Morgan)

The 'I1s' were built for use on prestigious passenger services between London and Brighton, but they later migrated to Tunbridge Wells services before being relegated to lesser duties by more-modern locomotives and then electrification. In terms of usage they were less flexible than the 0-6-0T and 0-6-2T types and as such would probably have been withdrawn by the 1940s had the war effort not necessitated their retention. Withdrawal nevertheless commenced in 1944, being completed in 1951, and none of the class achieved a million miles in service.

Atlantic tank N° 601 was completed in March 1907 and lasted until October 1948. It is seen here simmering away in one of the holding roads between Platforms 2 & 3 at East Croydon Station, waiting for its next turn of duty. (John Scott-Morgan)

I1 class 4-4-2 tank Atlantic N° 602 is seen here fully lined out in LB&SCR livery. It ended its days in June 1951, allocated to Bricklayers Arms depot. (John Scott-Morgan)

Completed in September 1907, Atlantic tank N° 32005 (originally numbered N° 5) was converted to become an I1X class less than a year later in August 1908. It was allocated to Brighton in BR days and was scrapped in June 1951. It is seen here in early British Railway livery. (John Scott-Morgan)

The Southern Railway, sometimes shortened to 'Southern', was established in the 1923 Grouping. The railway was formed by the amalgamation of several smaller railway companies, the largest of which were the London and South Western Railway (LSWR), the London, Brighton and South Coast Railway (LBSCR) and the South Eastern and Chatham Railway (SECR). At the grouping, the Southern initially maintained the locomotive numbers from its constituent company's and solved the problem of more than one locomotive having the same number by adding letter prefixes, denoting the main works of the former owning company. So that all ex-SECR locos were prefixed by an 'A' for Ashford, ex-LBSCR had a 'B' for Brighton and ex-LSWR engines had an 'E' for Eastleigh. In 1931 the fleet was re-numbered again, but this time all prefixes were dropped, leaving the E-prefixed numbers unchanged, adding 1000 to the A-prefixed numbers and adding 2000 to the B-prefixed ones. Here former LBSCR I1 class Atlantic tank N° 9 is seen at Brighton depot, resplendent in its new Southern livery of olive green, which it carried from 1924–1939, and had been introduced as the first standard passenger livery for the Southern Railway. (Author)

The I1s were never very popular with footplate crews, being consistently poor steamers. R. E. L. Maunsell decided to change them for the better and had the entire class re-boilered in the years 1923-32. The new boilers were taken from B4 4-4-0s when these were re-boilered as B4X locomotives; he also used boilers from I3s when these were superheated to become the I3X class. Upon rebuilding the I1s were reclassified I1X and in this form represented a great improvement over the original design. Maunsell also modified them to meet composite loading-gauge requirements, and they were fitted with new cabs similar to those of the Eastern Section's 2-6-4 tanks.

The Southern Railway initially added a 'B' prefix to the original numbers and later renumbered them as 2001-10 and 2595-2604. BR then added 30,000 to the numbers, although only N° 32005 actually ran in service with its new number. N° 2600 was the first to be withdrawn, being condemned in 1944. N° 2602 was used in the old 'Rooter' roundhouse at New Cross Gate depot during the late 1940s and was finally scrapped in June 1951. Eighteen members of the class survived long enough to pass into BR ownership in 1948, but all had been withdrawn by July 1951, and none was preserved.

The I2s

In 1907 Marsh sought to remedy some of the faults inherent in the I1 class with a new design of 4-4-2T featuring a longer wheelbase, larger boiler and detailed changes to the front end, and thus was born

the LBSCR's I2 class, designed for suburban passenger duties on the Brighton line. It was originally planned that, of the original order for 10 locomotives, five would have superheated boilers, to be supplied by the North British Locomotive Co, and five traditional saturated-steam boilers from Brighton Works. However, construction of the superheated boilers were delayed, so all 10 I2s had traditional boilers. When the superheated boilers did eventually arrive they were used for five further locomotives of broadly similar design, classified I4.

The I2 was essentially a larger version of the I1, but unfortunately the modifications did not address the fundamental problem with the I1 design — a firebox that was much too small. As a result the I2s, like the I1s, had relatively

short lives working lightly loaded secondary services, and the Stroudley D1s and Billinton D3s, which they had been designed to replace, remained in traffic.

The LBSCR numbered the 15 members of the I2 class as 11-20 and 31-5. When new N° 15 was given the honour of hauling the Royal Train taking King Edward VII from Victoria to see The Derby at Epsom Downs on 15 May 1908, while N° 19 was posed for the official photographer at the head of the stock for the new 'Southern Belle' service introduced the same year; restricted to a maximum load of five heavy Pullman cars, this was easily within the capability of the class, but later, as the loadings increased, its operation was taken over by H1 and H2 Atlantic tender engines.

Following the Grouping the

Following the failure of his I1 class, D. E. Marsh sought to remedy some of the faults with a new design of 4-4-2T. In the original order, five of the locomotives were to incorporate a superheated boiler supplied by the North British Locomotive Company. The remainder in the class were to have traditional saturated steam boilers, supplied by Brighton Works. In the end the superheated boilers were delayed in their construction and so all ten of the I2 class locomotives had traditional boilers fitted. Here N° 5 is seen in its later livery. (John Scott-Morgan)

Unfortunately the new I2 class engines did not address the problem encountered with the I1 class 4-4-2Ts in that the firebox was far too small. The I1 and I2 classes had short working lives after being put to use on lightly loaded secondary services. Here we see the first of the group, Nº 11, resplendent in a new coat of paint. (John Scott-Morgan)

The last numerical member of the I2 class was N° 35, which is seen here at Brighton depot with the abbreviated version of the owning company's name: the ampersand and 'R' have been removed. By this time the brakes, which had previously been fitted to the bogie, had been removed. (Author)

When the Southern Railway took over the I2 class of locomotives in 1923, it initially numbered them N° B11 - N° B20 and N° B31 - N° B35. The B denoted that they had originated from Brighton and was used to help distinguish engines operating on the Southern that had previously had the same operating number. Eventually, the class of I2 class Atlantics were renumbered again and became N° 2011 - N° 2020 and N° 2031 - N° 2035. Here N° B11 is seen glowing in the western afternoon sunshine at Battersea depot. In the background is a Pullman Brake vehicle of the 'Southern Belle' train, soon to be taken to Victoria Station, before it was worked once more back to Brighton. (Author)

WD locomotive Nº 72401 was formerly Brighton Atlantic tank Nº 2019 and is seen at Brighton c.1946. It was out of use by 1947. (John Scott-Morgan)

The LBSCR's B2 class was a batch of small 4-4-0 steam locomotives that acquired the nickname 'Grasshoppers' and were intended for express passenger work on the LBSCR's London to Portsmouth line. They were designed by R. J. Billinton and were built at Brighton Works from 1895 to 1897. They proved to be reliable locomotives but barely adequate for the heaviest trains. A member of the B2 class is seen working the 'Brighton Pullman Limited'. Many of the Pullman services on the Brighton line were taken over by the Brighton Atlantic tanks. (John Scott-Morgan)

L.B. & S.C.R. and L. & N.W.R. Liverpool to Brighton Express passing Wandsworth.

This contemporary image shows a Liverpool to Brighton inter-regional working. It was on one of these such workings that a superheated LBSC Atlantic tank I3 class locomotive would make a name for itself. Indeed, the LNWR were so impressed with its performance and low coal consumption that they would ultimately fit superheaters to their own locomotives. (John Scott-Morgan)

Southern Railway initially identified the I2s as B11-20 and B31-5; later they were renumbered 2011-20 and 2031-5. All were withdrawn between 1933 and 1939, but two, Nºs 2013 and 2019, saw further service on the Longmoor Military Railway in Hampshire, where they survived until at least 1947. Here they were numbered 2400 and 2401 respectively, although these numbers were later amended to 72400 and 72401. None of the class has been preserved.

Third time lucky! Here is the second in the batch of D. E. Marsh's very successful I3 class 4-4-2 tank Atlantic locomotive, Nº 22, resplendent in Brighton umber livery - the same colour as was used on the Pullman Cars. The I3 class was an excellent design which combined a great boiler, with a well-designed front end. This was thanks to B. K. Field, D. E. Marsh's right-hand man, and a fellow Swindon apprentice. (Author)

A **total** of 27 I3 class engines were produced. They all had 180lbs working pressure and the cylinder stroke in all cases was 26in, but the cylinder diameters showed some variation. The first of the engines to be built was given a 19in cylinder diameter, but this was increased to 21in in 1908 and early 1909 engines. The later 1909 and early 1910 products, of which Nº 29 was a member, reverted to the smaller diameter. Nº 29 seen here, was withdrawn in March 1951 from Tunbridge Wells West depot. (Author)

The I3s

Marsh's time at Brighton was not a period of unqualified success in terms of new locomotive designs, the best undoubtedly being the H1 Atlantic tender engine, which, of course, was based largely on a GNR design of H. A. Ivatt. By contrast his Atlantic tank engines of Classes I1 and I2 failed to impress, falling well short in terms of fulfilling the tasks for which they were built. Some of the locomotives that they were intended to replace eventually covered up to a million miles — far more than the Atlantic tanks ever did! In 1907, however, Marsh came up trumps, building the first of a very fine series of express tank engines for the Brighton line — the I3 4-4-2Ts.

Essentially a tank-engine version of Billinton's B4 4-4-0, the I3 was a very good design and considered superior to Churchward's contemporary 'County Tank' 4-4-2T on the GWR, combining an excellent boiler with well-designed front end designed by B. K. Field, a fellow Swindon apprentice and Marsh's right-hand man. It was, however, the addition of superheating that made the I3s noteworthy.

Marsh initially ordered two locomotives from Brighton Works to be built for comparative purposes, the first, Nº 21, being fitted with a traditional saturated boiler. All I3s had a working boiler pressure of 180lb, and in all cases the cylinder stroke was 26in, but the cylinder diameter showed some variation. Completed in October 1907, Nº 21 was given a 19in cylinder diameter, but this was increased to 21in in 1908. At around this time five new boilers fitted with Schmidt superheaters were constructed at Brighton, and the first of these was fitted to the second I3, turned out in March 1908. Nº 22 had 6ft 7½in wheels and 21x26in cylinders, and Marsh was persuaded by his chief draughtsman to fit the superheated boiler with an extended smokebox on a saddle. Although not the first superheated locomotive in

Britain (the Lancashire & Yorkshire Railway and the Great Western having each conducted experiments in this area) LBSCR No 22 was the first superheated express locomotive and without doubt the one which demonstrated that superheating was the way forward.

After several months of trials both locomotives were seen to be performing well and reliably. Nº 22 was found to be the more economical in terms of coal consumption as well as being a powerful performer on the heaviest of trains, but the LBSCR's directors were still not convinced that the extra building costs associated with superheating were matched by lower running costs. As a result four more superheated I3s (Nºs 23-6), were built in early 1909 and six more saturated versions (27-30, 75/6) in 1909/10 so that a truly fair comparison could be made between the saturated and superheated boilers.

Here is I3 class Atlantic tank Nº 29 which was completed in December 1909. It shared its time in BR days between Three Bridges and Tunbridge Wells and was withdrawn from service at Tunbridge Wells West, in March 1951. (John Scott-Morgan)

Here is N° 77, an I3 class Atlantic Tank seen at Battersea sheds being prepared for its next turn of duty. It was withdrawn from service when based at Eastbourne in March 1951. Note the driver with his large oil can and the massive builder's plate next to his leg. (John Scott-Morgan)

Here N° 78, an I3 Atlantic tank, is seen decked out in Royal Train regalia as it rests at Epsom Downs Station having worked the Royal train in from Victoria. It survived until March 1951 and was based at Three Bridges depot. On the right can be seen a rake of Pullman cars which had brought the expectant race goers to this 'must-see' event. (John Scott-Morgan)

Both varieties of I3 proved themselves to be excellent runners, but the superheated versions were significantly cheaper to run on express trains, consuming just 30lb of coal per mile, compared with the 36, 40 and 42lb respectively of the saturated I3s, H1s and B4s. They were capable of operating the heaviest of LBSCR express services over all routes without difficulty and could cover the 84 miles from Clapham Junction to Fratton in 1hr 40min non-stop, despite having a water capacity of just 2,110 gallons. It was, however, further afield that the merits of the design would be most graphically demonstrated.

Introduced in July 1904 as a joint venture with the London & North Western Railway, the 'Sunny South Express' included through carriages from Liverpool, Manchester and Birmingham to Brighton and Eastbourne. From July 1905, in partnership with the South Eastern & Chatham Railway, the LNWR introduced a through service from Liverpool to Folkestone and Dover, and later one from Manchester to Deal. Generally the 'Sunny South Express' ran daily between May and September and on Saturdays in the winter period, and in some years the Eastbourne portion continued to Hastings. For many years the train was worked between Willesden and the South Coast by an LBSCR B2 or B4 on the Sussex route and by an SECR D1 or E1 4-4-0 on the Kent portion, but it was an example of the I3 class which in 1909 was used in a series of comparative trials. The LNWR was keen to test its 'Precursor' 4-4-0s, and one of these, N° 7 *Titan*, was pitted against one of the LBSCR 4-4-2Ts, with dramatic results — in favour of the tank engine. In one trial N° 23 worked the train through from Willesden Junction to Rugby non-stop, much to the astonishment of the LNWR, which usually provided two locomotives for this duty, loaded to a fairly light 250 tons!

Although not unaware of the other qualities demonstrated by the I3s, other railways were most interested in the fact that they consumed considerably less coal and water than did the 'Precursors'. A superheated I3 could leave Brighton with its coal bunker containing some 3¼ tons of coal and take the 'Sunny South Express' to Rugby and back without any need for water *en route* or re-coaling at Rugby, an amazing performance of about 27lb per mile, assuming that no coal was remaining in

A southbound '*Sunny South Express' is* seen at Addison Road, Kensington, made up of LNWR elliptical roof stock headed by a member of the LBSCR's Gladstone B1 class 0-4-2 N° 172. A tall LNWR three-doll bracket signal stands on the left. (L&NWR Society Image N° SOC 598)

London & North Western Railway Precursor class 4-4-0 N° 7 *Titan* is seen standing at Brighton Station with the northbound '*Sunny South Express*', made up of LNWR elliptical roof carriages. Notice the LBSCR head code symbols fitted on the locomotives lamp sockets. The engine was taking part in C. J. B. Cooke's locomotive interchange trials and is seen on 22 January 1910. (L&NWR Society Image N° JFW 712)

London & North Western Railway 4-4-0 Precursor Nº 7 *Titan* is setting off with an up-express at Crewe. The first five carriages are 'arc roof' bogies followed by a clerestory diner. When *Titan* was working the *'Sunny South Express'* it would have worked from Rugby through to Brighton. A Whitworth 2-4-0 locomotive is seen alongside on the right. (L&NWR Society Image Nº SOCA 1244)

Seen on 22 January 1910, London & North Western Railway 4-4-0 Precursor Nº 1516 *Alecto* stands at Willesden north. Well-coaled and standing to the north west of the station, it is ready to take over the *'Sunny South Express'* from the LBSCR's 4-4-0 Nº 73, which had just arrived with the train from Brighton. The train, which is made up of LNWR stock, is just about to be uncoupled. The over-bridge carrying Old Oak Lane is seen in the background and a cattle dock can be seen adjacent to *Alecto*'s buffer beam, on the left. (L&NWR Society Image Nº JFW 701)

the bunker when it arrived back at Brighton. Significantly, the LNWR's next design of passenger locomotive, the 'George the Fifth' 4-4-0, incorporated a Schmidt superheater. The 'Precursors' also ran against the GNR's large-boiler Atlantics, trials being conducted on each company's main line using each type of locomotive, and again the LNWR type did not show up well in terms of economy.

By mid-1910 there was sufficient operating data to convince the LBSCR's directors that hereafter all locomotives should be superheated. Later that year five more superheated I3s appeared as N°s 77-81, these also featuring the larger-diameter cylinders introduced on N° 22. Altogether 27 I3s were produced, 10 more superheated examples being constructed in 1912 and 1913 under the auspices of L. B. Billinton following Marsh's departure. Numbered 82-91, they all had cylinders of 21in diameter. These differed from the earlier locomotives in that they were provided with a vacuum brake (which would make them very useful for working ambulance trains during the First World War); they also had different feed pumps and higher cab roofs and lacked superheater dampers.

After the war Billinton wished to fit the remaining saturated I3s with superheaters as their boilers became due for renewal, but only the prototype N° 21 was so treated before the LBSCR merged with other railways to form the Southern Railway in January 1923. The remaining locomotives were finally superheated between 1925 and

L. J. Billinton built the last ten of the I3 class engines from 1912-1913 and numbered them N° 82 - N° 91. Fitted with superheaters and larger cylinders, these engines were a development from D. E. Marsh's design. Here, N° 83 is seen at Brighton depot with abbreviated ownership branding on its water tank sides. (Author)

1927, their original, saturated-steam boilers being rebuilt in superheated form by Maunsell, who used his own design of superheater. Later new, superheated boilers were provided for the I3s, releasing serviceable B4-type boilers which were then used by Maunsell in rebuilding the I1s as Class I1X; further B4 boilers were made available by rebuilding the B4s themselves as B4X locomotives, with 'K'-class Belpaire boilers.

During 1925/6 the I3s were replaced on London–Brighton expresses by 'King Arthur' 4-6-0s and 'River' 2-6-4Ts, being relegated to semi-fast and other secondary services. They were also cut down slightly, by reducing the height of the boiler mountings and 'rounding-off' the profile of the cab roofs, to allow them to work on the Eastern Section to Dover. Subsequently I3s moved further afield, four examples being allocated to Salisbury from 1938 to work trains thence to Portsmouth. The Southern Railway initially added a B (for Brighton) prefix to their numbers, later renumbering them as 2021-30 and 2075-91.

During the Second World War two I3s were loaned to the GWR. No 2091 went first to Gloucester before moving on to Worcester, where it replaced a '45xx' tank engine and, for example, worked the 5am service to Moreton-in-Marsh, the 1.15pm and 4.27pm services to Leamington and also on the Stourbridge locals. The Western men found N° 2091 — and N° 2089, which joined it from Gloucester — to be comparable with their '51xx' 2-6-2 tanks. By the end of 1942 N° 2091 was out of regular use, although it was sent to retrieve a failed 'Bulldog' 4-4-0. By March 1943 both I3s were at Gloucester,

One of the two works plates that were fitted to I3 class Atlantic tank N° 86, constructed at the LB&SCR's Brighton Works in 1912. The locomotive was then first renumbered as N° B086 in Southern Railway days, before becoming 2086 and was finally renumbered as N° 32086 in British Railways days. It was finally withdrawn from service at Brighton in October 1951. (Author)

where N° 2091, sometimes appeared on the Cheltenham–Kingham services. Both locomotives returned to the Southern in July 1943.

The first member of the class to be withdrawn was N° 2024, condemned by the Southern Railway in 1944, but the remainder passed into BR stock, being renumbered 32021/30 and 32075-91. Most were withdrawn during 1950/1, replaced by new LMS-designed and BR Standard '4MT' 2-6-4 tanks, but last-built N° 32091 survived until in June 1952, when it was withdrawn with a final mileage of 1,401,271. This was not the end, however, as, after a period in store, it was cleaned up for display at the Brighton Works Centenary celebrations held in the autumn of 1952, being exhibited along with

Southern liveried I3 class 4-4-2T Atlantic N° 2088 is seen resting between duties at Stewarts Lane depot. Completed at Brighton Works during November 1912, it was allocated to Brighton depot in 1947 and again in 1950, from where it was withdrawn from service and scrapped at Brighton Works in November 1950. (Author)

N° 32086 at Brighton on 24 July 1948. It is seen here in British Railways livery, with a drop shadow incorporated into the lettering and numbering. (John Scott-Morgan)

Freshly painted N° 32022 is seen on 7 October 1950. It was built in March 1908 and lasted until May 1951 allocated at Tunbridge Wells West depot. (John Scott-Morgan)

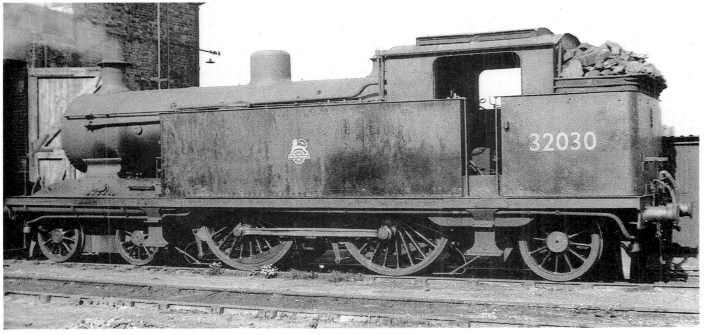

Class 'I3' N° 32030 seen at Eastbourne depot. It carries the earlier BR lion and wheel insignia, which first appeared on GWR Castle class locomotive N° 7018 *Drysllwyn Castle* in May 1949. (John Scott-Morgan)

The last numerical member of its class, Nº 32091, is seen at Brighton depot on 24 June 1952; the month it was withdrawn from service. (John Scott-Morgan)

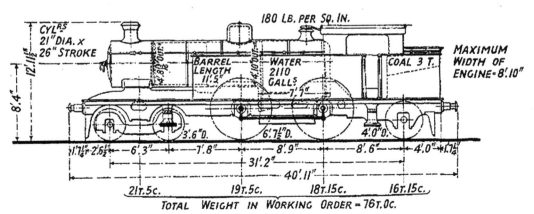

An official drawing of the LBSCR I3 class 4-4-2T Atlantic locomotives. (Author)

HEATING SURFACE, TUBES—								
LARGE AND SMALL	...	...	...	...	1,126·0 SQ. FT.
FIREBOX	...	...	...	...	120·0 ,,
TOTAL (EVAPORATIVE)	...	...	...	1,246·0 ,,
SUPERHEATER	...	...	...	...	254·0 ,,
COMBINED HEATING SURFACES	...	...	1,500·0 ,,

SUPERHEATER ELEMENTS	...	...	...	21–1⅜ IN. DIA. OUTS.
LARGE TUBES	...	... 21–4½ IN. DIA. OUTS. ⎱	11 FT. 2⁷⁄₁₆ IN.
SMALL TUBES	...	...162–1¾ IN. DIA. OUTS. ⎰	BET. TUBEPLATES
GRATE AREA	...	...	...	23·75 SQ. FT.
TRACTIVE EFFORT (AT 85 PER CENT. B.P.)	...	...	22,100 LB.

'A1X' 0-6-0T No 32640, formerly named *Brighton*, and 'Schools' 4-4-0 No 30915 *Brighton*.

Regrettably none of these ground-breaking locomotives survived the cutter's torch, Nº 32091 being scrapped in January 1953 at Ashford Works and thereby achieving the dubious distinction of becoming the first ex-LBSCR express passenger locomotive to be cut up there.

I4 class

In 1908 Marsh attempted to follow the success of his I3 tanks with another 4-4-2T design, the I4, which was essentially a superheated I2. The class comprised five locomotives, Nº s 31-5, fitted with 17½x26in cylinders and small boilers (1,098ft total heating surface) set to 160lb pressure. Of broadly similar design to the I2s, they were no more successful. It was thus proved that superheating alone was not the answer to success as had appeared to be the case with the I3s, and the I4s proved a big disappointment. Following the Grouping there was a proposal to rebuild them along the lines of the I1X'rebuilds of the I1 class, but in the end the decision was taken to scrap them, and all bar one had been withdrawn by the end of 1937. The exception, Nº 2034, survived in traffic until May 1940, and after it had been cut up its boiler was repaired and sent to Fleet; there it was used to supply steam to an air-compressor providing a means of operating signalling on the South Western main line, being reported still in use in November 1948. The boiler of another I4 (which avoided scrapping until September 1940) was sold to the Sussex & Dorking Brick Co, which used it until 1949.

The LBSCR's I4 class 4-4-2T Atlantic locomotive Nº 31, the first member of the class, seen at Battersea depot. In the background, over the boiler, can be seen part of the LBSCR's over-head electrification system gantry, which sat on the viaduct. (John Scott-Morgan)

Here I4 class 4-4-2T Atlantic locomotive N° 35 is seen in LBSC livery. It entered service in February 1909 and was withdrawn in February 1937. (John Scott-Morgan)

Here is the former LBSCR I4 class 4-4-2T Atlantic locomotive N° 32, as seen in Southern Railway days when it was numbered N° 2032. It is seen dumped at Eastleigh on 9 April 1938, having been withdrawn from service in July 1937. (John Scott-Morgan)

I4 class 4-4-2T Atlantic locomotive Nº 2033 in Southern Railway livery is seen withdrawn and dumped in Eastleigh yard. It entered traffic in November 1908 and was withdrawn in July 1937. (John Scott-Morgan)

Built in December 1908, this I4 class 4-4-2T locomotive, originally numbered as Nº 34, was never taken into British Railways stock. It was re-numbered Nº 2034 under Southern Railway and withdrawn from service in May 1940. (Author)

The LBSCR I4 class 4-4-2T Atlantic locomotive entered service as N° 35, becoming N° B035 in Southern Railway days and then finally N° 2035. It is seen as SR N° 2035 at Eastleigh on 30 May 1937. (John Scott-Morgan)

Chapter 12

RE-CREATING N° 32424 *BEACHY HEAD*

Regrettably no Brighton Atlantic survived long enough to be preserved, but remarkably not one but two boilers from GNR 'Large Atlantics', the design of which the Brighton locomotives closely followed, were discovered in the late 1980s in Essex, where they had survived in use at a timber-drying plant. The discovery prompted a group to re-create one of the long-lost Brighton Atlantics, and one of the boilers was duly purchased by the Bluebell Railway, which set about building a replica of H2 N° 32424 *Beachy Head*. Reproduced below are the notes of Nick Pigott, former Editor of *The Railway Magazine*, in which he describes how events unfolded.

'Early in 1986 a fellow enthusiast and I decided to form the Engine Shed Society to cater for the interests of "rail-fans" interested in locomotive depots and their allocations.

'One of the first things we needed to establish was how many steam sheds still stood in Britain and what use they had been put to since closure. For the major city MPDs this was common knowledge in most cases, but for the many tiny rural depots and sub-sheds it necessitated long expeditions by car to investigate sites at first hand.

'On one such trip around East Anglia we arrived at the small Essex town of Maldon one Saturday evening, just before dusk, and began investigating the area behind the disused station. It became clear that the site of the former shed lay close to an old abandoned factory complex. We cautiously looked around and then, after taking a few paces, stopped dead in our tracks. For there, just out of public sight, were the unmistakable outlines of four steam railway locomotives! It was the nearest thing to 'buried treasure' a steam enthusiast could find.

'As our eyes became accustomed to the shadows we realised that they were boilers only, but the profiles of two of them were making our pulses quicken, for we both swore blind that they were Great Northern Railway Atlantics. The other two were much smaller and appeared to have come from six-coupled tank engines or similar.

'It was too dark to take photos — this was the pre-digital age — but there was just enough light left to see what we were doing, so I rushed back to the car to get a tape measure and took the vital dimensions of length, smokebox radius etc in order to check up once we got home. With the help of a torch I found a small set of identifying numbers on one of the boilers.

'The following week, having ascertained that the dimensions tallied with those of GNR 32-element-superheater boilers, I made a phone call to Hull and spoke to W. B. (Willie) Yeadon, the veteran compiler of LNER locomotive histories, to tell him of the find. He was as astonished as I was and said he would consult his reference documents. He duly rang back to say that the reference number I had given him identified it as a boiler that had been fitted to LNER "C1" 4-4-2 N° 3278 between August 1943 and October 1945.

'Several boilers had been sold in the late 1940s by Doncaster and Stratford Works for use as stationary boilers in private industry, but for some of them, including the one off N° 3278, the trail had then gone cold, as the official LNER records had not recorded to whom they were sold.

'Once I had alerted the heritage railway world to the discovery,

With all of the original LBSCR Atlantics long gone, and the discovery of a former GNR C1 class Atlantic boiler at an Essex factory, a plan was formed to rebuild Nº 32424 *Beachy Head* and get it back on the rails within sixty years of its last steaming. Here is the boiler waiting to be lifted onto the frames at Sheffield Park. (Author)

several engineers made their way to coastal Essex to take a look at the boilers and assess their condition. This resulted in all four being rescued and moved to other locations.

'Sadly one of the Atlantic boilers was later scrapped by a firm based at nearby Brightlingsea, but its classmate — which, it has subsequently been discovered, is boiler Nº 9359, once fitted to loco Nº 3287 — was moved to the Bluebell Railway, Sussex, to form the basis of a new-build LBSCR Marsh Atlantic, Nº 32424 *Beachy Head*.'

Thus it was that on 29 October 2000 the Bluebell Railway announced its intention to reconstruct *Beachy Head*, painted in BR lined-black livery and with the number 32424, using many of the surviving H2 parts as possible, it having been decided that the locomotive should be a 'rebuild' as opposed to a 'new build'. Below are the notes of David Jones, C.Eng, M.I.Mech.E., Secretary and Treasurer of the Atlantic Project, outlining what has been achieved so far.

It had always been regretted by many railway enthusiasts that

none of the LBSCR 'K'-class Moguls or H1/H2 Atlantics had been preserved, this being due mainly to fact that these locomotives were scrapped prior to the establishment of the railway-preservation movement, initiated by the Talyllyn on the narrow gauge in 1950 and the Bluebell and Middleton railways on the standard gauge in 1960. There were attempts at preserving examples of both these large LBSCR classes, but they came to nothing. Therefore, when in 1986, Nick Pigott and his colleagues discovered four stationary boilers at a woodworking factory in Maldon, Essex, two of them from GNR 'Large Atlantics', there was a glimmer of hope that reconstructing a Marsh version might be feasible. Although there were two boilers, together with a further two smaller examples (later identified as being from LSWR and MGNR locomotives), only one GNR version was in good condition.

All four boilers were purchased by Shipyard Services of Brightlingsea and had their blue asbestos removed, then metal surfaces were grit blasted and painted prior to being offered for sale. After an inspection by Bluebell Railway locomotive engineers, who were really after a boiler for the LSWR Adams 'radial tank', the better GNR one was purchased in 1987 for £12,727 and transported by road to Sheffield Park in anticipation of a long-term project to build a replica LBSCR Atlantic, so re-creating a 'lost' locomotive. It has subsequently been identified as one of a batch of five spare boilers constructed in 1943 and fitted to GNR locomotive No 3287 but was

The LBSCR 4-4-2 Atlantics were built to drawings modified from the Great Northern Railway large boiler design, and so the boiler is entirely correct for the new *Beachy Head* engine. Here, boiler Nº 9359, once fitted to loco Nº 3287, is seen in Atlantic House during an 'Open-Day' in 2013. (Author)

used for only two years prior to sale for industrial use at Maldon.

Because the Bluebell Railway was heavily involved in restoring a number of ex-Barry scrapyard locomotives at the time, the Atlantic scheme had to take a back seat until the end of 2000, when Terry Cole, Chairman of the Bluebell Railway Preservation Society at the time of purchase of the boiler, decided to recruit a small team of skilled volunteers and start the reconstruction in earnest. Keith Sturt and Fred Bailey became the key players in this scheme, and without them the project would not have got off the ground. During the period between the purchase of the boiler and the effective start of the reconstruction it had been possible

to acquire a tender under-frame from the LBSCR's B4-class 4-4-0 Nº 63 *Pretoria* and a set of three wheel and axle-box assemblies from an LBSCR C2X 0-6-0 locomotive that had been used at the now-closed 'Empire and Railways' display at Windsor & Eton station. The restoration of the tender was therefore put in hand whilst funds were raised to source and purchase the locomotive frames and wheels. A glossy appeal leaflet, funded by the Bluebell Railway Trust, was circulated to all members of the Bluebell Railway Preservation Society, and the positive response allowed a start to be made on the reconstruction. The standing-order scheme, usually a contribution of £15 per quarter, is still running

strongly, although, sadly, many of the initial subscribers have now passed away.

The Project Team decided to name the new-build locomotive *Beachy Head*, effectively re-creating perhaps the most famous of the Marsh Atlantics on account of its

Components for the Bluebell Railway's Atlantic *Beachy Head* project waiting to be machined in the summer of 2013. The item on the left is a part-machined eccentric for the Stephenson Valve-Gear and the one on the right is an eccentric strap in its as-cast condition. (Author)

Here are the four eccentrics, machined from 'free-issued' castings by TMA Ltd, Birmingham. The top one on this stack is separated slightly to show the joint between the two halves. They have all been machined and inspected to well within the drawing tolerances. (Fred Bailey)

One of the four eccentric straps, machined by TMA Ltd, Birmingham, from 'free-issue' castings. (Fred Bailey)

being the last to remain in traffic, until April 1958; an earlier idea of taking the next number, 427, and naming the locomotive after another headland (suggested by many as *Seven Sisters*) was abandoned. A start was made on overhauling and modifying the tender chassis,

which had been purchased in September 1991 from the group restoring 'Battle of Britain' Pacific N° 34070 *Manston* from 'Barry' condition, but the work being tackled outside in all weathers highlighted the need for a building of some sort. After overcoming problems identifying a space in the Sheffield Park Works yard and with financial assistance from the Bluebell Railway Trust again, a lightweight structure measuring 10m by 20m was purchased in kit form and erected over the winter of 2005/6. This was following frustrating delays with planning permission, granted in December 2004, Building Control Regulations and poor instructions for the erection of the flat-pack structure. Eventually, after modifications were made to the design including insulating the building, the appropriately named 'Atlantic House' was officially opened by Richard Gibbon OBE, previously at the National Railway Museum, on 11 June 11 2006. A big surprise at this event was the unexpected presentation by John Wiseman of the regulator handle from the original *Beachy Head* that he had purchased just after the locomotive had been scrapped. The team wondered if there were any more of the original out there. There was, because, having heard about the Atlantic Project, Ethel Kefford contacted the team and offered the original whistle which had been bought by her late husband, who was employed in the Accounts Office at Brighton Works. This was duly presented by her at the 2008 Open Weekend celebrating 50 years since the original locomotive was

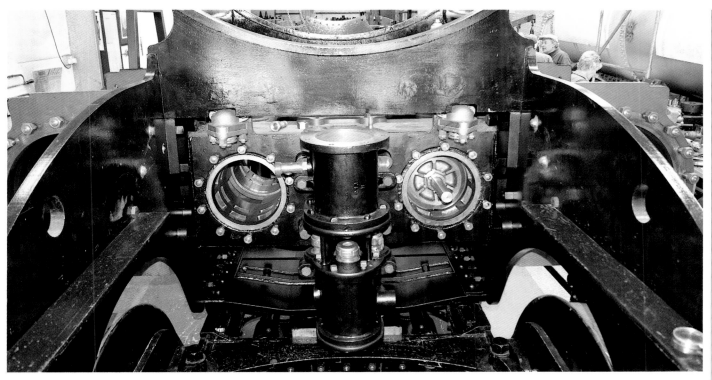

View showing the frames resting on the bogie and trailing wheel-sets. The two valve chests, as well as the two brass anti-vacuum valves located just under the smokebox saddle, can be seen. (Author)

scrapped and which coincided with a 'Built at Brighton' weekend on the Bluebell.

Several years earlier the two Bluebell pattern-makers had offered their services and had been tasked with making those for the bogie and driving-wheel centres. With a very generous donation from the late Peter Cox, these were cast in steel by Norton Cast Products of Sheffield in 2003 and subsequently sent to Riley's of Bury to be pressed onto axles and for tyres to be fitted, both these latter items having to be imported from South Africa. Although the bogie wheels were dealt with fairly quickly, it was never anticipated that the large 6ft 7½in driving and coupled wheels would take over five years, eventually arriving as complete wheel-sets early in 2013.

Another frustrating episode surrounded the main-frame plates. These had been drawn up using computer-aided design methods and readily sponsored by two keen supporters at £2,750 each, but Corus could only cut the profile and not put the joggle or 'set' into them. Efforts were made to find a suitable company with a large press, approaches being made to firms in the North of England and in Scotland, including shipyards, but all enquiries drew a blank. Eventually the firm of Pridhams in Devon — now incorporated into the South Devon Railway works — was able to carry out this bending task on its 700-ton press, ex-Crewe Works. The correctly profiled and joggled frames were delivered to Sheffield Park on 29 November 2005 to be lifted off the delivery

lorry with the same crane that had positioned the boiler and tender chassis onto the concrete pad that would eventually have the shell of 'Atlantic House' erected over it.

Once the building had been erected and fitted out with shelving and a pillar crane, kindly donated by a local company that had no further use for it, the main

This image of the driving wheel-sets clearly shows the unusual eccentric crankpin. The leading wheel-set, with a much smaller balance weight, is seen on the right. (Author)

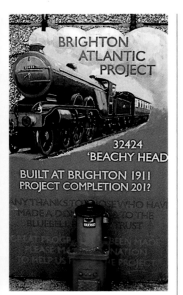

Hung on a wall outside the steam shed at Sheffield Park depot, is a poster that says it all. (Author)

frames could be drilled with the numerous holes for attaching horn-guides, frame stretchers, cylinders and many other components. On 1 October 2007, amid great secrecy, the frames were erected vertically and braced together, officially creating the new *Beachy Head*.

In the meantime a team of Atlantic Group members and colleagues from other sections of the Bluebell's locomotive department were on a mission to obtain copies of the original drawings, some of which were thought to exist at the National Railway Museum in York but were stored in their basement with no catalogue or indication of how many survived. A series of week-long visits over three years resulted in about 50 of a set of 270 drawings of the Atlantic being found, together with those for other locomotives on the Bluebell. These were used to produce detail drawings on a Computer Aided Design system which have subsequently been invaluable for manufacturing most of the components including the wheels, frame stretchers, weigh-shaft brackets, sandboxes and most importantly the unusual air-assisted reverser mechanism in the cab. The manufacture of this device with a four-start square thread was entrusted to TMA in Birmingham, a well-known supplier of specialist parts for locomotives. Another outside contractor used by the Atlantic Project was Unilathe of Stoke-on-Trent, which is certified for the main-line railway industry and also a sub-contractor for JCB. It has supplied many parts including the extension rods for the

Stephenson valve mechanism made from forgings.

Mention of forgings brings to mind the subject of connecting rods and coupling rods. In the past such items would have been readily available from British industry; indeed the connecting rods for the Maunsell Locomotive Society's 'Q'-class 0-6-0, N° 541, were forged at Anderson Bros of Coatbridge, and those for 'U'class 2-6-0 N° 1638 at Hesketh's of Bury. However, both firms have since closed, so an alternative idea using forged billets of EN19 steel, which can still be purchased, then water-jet cut the shapes was considered. This route was therefore taken and the billets, cut to shape by a firm in Crowborough and delivered in December 2008, were subsequently machined and fluted at a foundry in Stourport. Interestingly a number of other locomotive preservation and new-build groups, both in the UK and overseas, have contacted the 'Atlantic' team with a view to producing such rods by this method.

The main axle-boxes were delivered in 2009 but would have to wait until the main wheels were received before the final white-metal machining could be done at Sheffield Park.

The second area requiring a re-think was the manufacture of the cylinder and valve-chest assembly, as both the pattern and casting of a combined component to the original design would have been prohibitively expensive. An alternative, based on US locomotive practice, was chosen which was to fabricate them as three parts, the outside two cylinders and a central

double valve chest. Following the water-jet production of all the ribs and back plates, the whole lot was welded together by Keith Sturt and sent away to be normalised at 630?C in order to stress-relieve the welds ready for final machining. Once returned to Sheffield Park, their respective liners were inserted, the cylinder ones being secured with a very expensive high temperature Loctite adhesive. The three assemblies were fitted in the spring of 2012 and then subjected to a leak test to prove the Hulburds copper seals, these being a copy of a design introduced for steam locomotives a century ago and made by EPAL in Storrington. This firm also later made the axlebox crowns and the expansion link and die block, both using the wire eroding method which gives a very fine and accurate dimensional finish. It should be emphasised at this point that all the outside contracting companies mentioned here are not necessarily recommended by the Atlantic Project.

At the same time attention had been focussed on assembling the leading bogie following receipt the small front wheels from Riley's in October 2010, so allowing the bronze axle-boxes to be machined to suit. This was in order to reward the valued supporters of the project when they attended the annual Open Weekend on 23/24 June 2012, as by then the locomotive was a rolling chassis for the first time, albeit without the main driving wheels, still awaited from Riley's! This exercise involved lifting the locomotive 18 inches off the ground using individual standard hydraulic jacks, in order to run the bogie and the rear trailing wheel-set underneath. It was mentioned that when the driving wheels eventually arrive a similar lift, but up to 4ft would be required so a more substantial jacking system would be needed. In the meantime many castings were arriving from Cerdic of Chard including the sandboxes and covers, plus new valve heads and rings from the Severn Valley Railway.

The Bluebell's pattern-makers had started on the large and complicated superheater header which would take several months of their time. Many of the smaller pins, special bolts, shafts and joints have been made in 'Atlantic House' on the centre lathe, and the milling machine was used to manufacture all sorts of brackets, oilers, support assemblies and greasing points for the locomotive.

The Atlantic team also includes expert machinists who have produced many fine components over the years using experience gained from their earlier days as apprentices in the Bluebell Railway Works, and others are very handy with the paintbrush on the numerous castings and other parts.

A review of the financial position early in 2013 revealed that the standing order income, mainly from members of the Bluebell Railway Preservation Society had now exceeded £2,000 a month, and income from the sponsorship of components had passed £185,000 with a total of over £700,000 from all donations since the project started. Based on future expenditure, it was estimated that an additional £250,000 would be required so

resulting in a final total of £1 million for the new *Beachy Head*.

At about this time thoughts were being given to constructing a bespoke lifting frame, so following the drawing up of an in-house design and checking the loading calculations verified by a Test engineer with experience within British Rail, the relevant substantial steelwork and heavy-duty Enerpac hydraulic jacks were ordered. The individual sections of the lifting frame were then welded together and painted in the required bright yellow, after which the whole assembly was overload tested and a trial lift of a few inches was carried out.

Although activity was concentrated on the components associated with the main locomotive frame assembly, especially the Stephenson valve gear, the ex-GNR boiler was not forgotten as much had to be done on fitting additional pipework peculiar to the LBSCR version, and inspecting the foundation ring area where corrosion usually takes place. A full ultrasonic test was carried out earlier which indicated a need to replace one or two stays and parts of the corroded boiler plate around the foundation ring. New steel sections, water-jet cut, were made for welding into the areas where replacements were needed. It was also necessary to tap out the copper firebox tube-plate for the flue tubes, which was done using a long tube as a guide to make sure the threads were square to the plates. The plan being to complete the boiler whilst it is still in 'Atlantic House', then move it outside for hydraulic and steam tests before fitting it

into the frames. Final fitting work and painting will probably be done in the main Bluebell Works where the overhead cranes will be essential.

At the time of writing, the anticipated completion date is around 2018, but this will depend on continuing financial support and availability of skilled labour and the correct materials. There are no plans to use the locomotive on the main line, it having always been intended as an additional flagship for use on the extended Bluebell Railway, joining the impressive range of Southern-area locomotives dating from 1872 until the end of Southern steam in 1967.

Significant milestones have been as follows:

- GNR Atlantic boiler obtained
- LBSCR B4 tender chassis obtained
- LBSCR C2X tender wheel-sets and axle-boxes obtained
- Wheels for trailing wheel-set obtained
- Tender chassis overhauled and lengthened (2001-5)
- Bogie plate-work delivered (December 2004)
- 'Atlantic House' constructed — the project has a home (2005/6)
- Driving and bogie wheels cast (2005)
- Main frames cut, joggled and delivered (2005)
- Original regulator handle from N° 32424 donated to the project (2006)
- Tender chassis re-wheeled (2006)
- Westinghouse pump obtained

- Main frames erected (October 2007)
- Cylinder and valve-chest components delivered (July 2008)
- First motion parts water-jet cut from forged blanks (April 2009)
- Bogie frames assembled (2009)
- Valve chest assembly welded together; main axle-boxes delivered (spring 2010)
- Bogie and trailing wheel-sets completed; cylinders fabricated (autumn 2010)
- Coupling and connecting rods machined and delivered; rear cylinder covers cast (early 2011)
- Axle-boxes completed, with manganese steel liners and oil trays; smokebox saddle fabricated (mid-2011)
- Cab reverser completed; valve heads cast (late 2011)

- Valve and cylinder liners fitted (early 2012)
- Frames supported on bogie and trailing truck (mid-2012)
- Valve chest and cylinders fitted to frames; covers fitted and pressure-tested (2012)

Main wheel-sets completed and delivered (March 2013)

Lifting frames constructed and commissioned (May 2013)

Much of the valve gear assembled. Slide bars aligned (August 2013)

Last major valve gear components delivered (December 2013)

Weigh (reversing) shaft and air-clutch fitted (January 2014)

Axle-boxes metalled, machined and fitted (February 2014)

Wheel Rotators constructed (February 2014)

Eccentric rods fitted (March 2014)

Most work between the frames (valve and reversing gear, pipework for brakes and steam heat) completed. Locomotive wheeled (May 2014)

Cylinders clad, crossheads fitted, superheater-header casting patterns completed (August 2014)

Bogie and inside motion completed, giving us a rolling chassis (May 2015)

Running plates, with splashers and steps, completed (June 2015)

Cylinder covers fitted, cab floor, sides and front assembled (October 2015)

Connecting and coupling rods fitted, valves set (February 2016)

Work on mud holes completed (December 2016)

A model of D. E. Marsh's H2 class 4-4-2 Atlantic *Beachy Head* as it was during Southern Railway days. (Author) (*Courtesy of The Brighton Toy & Model Museum, Brighton*)

EPILOGUE

Richard H. N. Hardy was born in 1923 and was educated at Marlborough College, as indeed was Sir Nigel Gresley. Richard served an apprenticeship at Doncaster Works and Carr Loco shed between 1941 and 1944. He then spent a further 38 years working in the railway industry. He served in East Anglia and was Shedmaster at Woodford Halse from the autumn of 1949, after which he moved to Stewarts Lane depot and became the Shed Master there between August 1952 to January 1955. He then moved on to the Stratford District in general and Stratford depot in particular as Assistant District Motive Power Superintendent. SNCF experiences on the Nord and Est regions were obtained between 1958 and 1971, and one of his last jobs was Divisional Manager at Liverpool, on the London Midland Region. He retired in 1982. The author of *Steam in the Blood* (1971), *Railways in the Blood* (1985) and *Beeching — Champion of the Railway?* (1989), he has also written numerous articles about railways as well the Introduction to *The Railwayman's Pocket Book*. Reproduced below are his thoughts on the Brighton Atlantics.

Douglas Earle Marsh was responsible for the design of the Brighton Atlantic express passenger locomotive. He had been H. A. Ivatt's Works Manager at Doncaster on the Great Northern Railway, and when he arrived at Brighton as Locomotive Engineer he found that some more powerful passenger locomotives were required and quickly … and what better than to ask for a set of drawings of the Ivatt Atlantics from his erstwhile boss. But they would not quite fit the bill without some common-sense alterations such as larger cylinders and higher boiler pressure. But when they were superheated it was a 24-element superheater that was fitted, whereas on the Great Northern the 32-element superheater was eventually adopted, which turned the GNR engines into world-beaters. So when the Brighton Atlantic now being reconstructed at Sheffield Park eventually takes up its duties (it has a GN Atlantic's boiler pressed at 170lb, a 32-element superheater and the larger cylinders), what a machine that could turn out to be.

In passing it must be said that Marsh's contribution to the locomotive stock of his railway was quite remarkable. For suburban work he created the I1, I2 and I4 classes. They were poor, under-boilered, shy-steaming affairs, yet they were broadly based on the GN 'C12s', on which I worked from time to time and which threw the fire but would steam and run very freely. The C3 goods engines went back almost to the Dark Ages, but the I3 tank engines were superheated and brilliant and spoken of very fondly, not only by drivers who had grown up with them but by the firemen who had passed through the LBSC links at my predominantly SECR shed,

A view of Dick Hardy taken in 1929, when he was about 6 years old: he had been invited to a fancy dress party and dressed up as an engine driver. His mother had spoken to the local Station Master at Leatherhead, who had promptly taken her along to the platforms where a driver was happy to oblige in taking down measurements for Dick's uniform. Dick was presented with an oil-feeder and is seen complete with a sponge cloth sticking out of his pocket. (R. H. N. Hardy)

Dick Hardy (on the right) with driver Harry Moyer posing on 0-6-0 tender engine N° 4040 at Grantham, in September 1941. The engine was built in 1896 and had a genuine Stirling curved topped cab. This was one of the many different types of engines that Dick gained experience on in his formative years as a fireman. (R. H. N. Hardy)

Stewarts Lane, where I only just missed them.

Algy Harman was one of our running foremen and had transferred from the LBSC depot of Battersea Park when it was closed in 1935; he had fired on both classes and had a useful tip for those who would champion the cause of scientific firing. At Battersea Park they used the very best Welsh coal on the more difficult jobs, and the fireman of a heavy 60-minute train would fill the firebox of his Atlantic at the shed and let it get well burnt through by the time the train was due away from Victoria.

The fireman would lift the fire with the poker and sit down on his apology of a seat. He looked after the water level in the boiler but never touched the fire until well past Haywards Heath, whereupon he would have a look round, level it with the fire-iron and run quietly into Brighton on time. This was not textbook firing but perfectly acceptable unless for some reason both injectors failed *en route* and the fire had to be thrown out; I recall this happening one Sunday evening during the war with a noble Gresley A1, N° 2555 *Centenary*, when the fire had to be dropped short of

Ardsley Tunnel — a murderous business, but, of course, most of our Gresley and Thompson locomotives had a drop grate and maybe a hopper ashpan which made life easier for everyone bar the local ganger and his men! And there are quite a few photographs of GN Atlantics on the pre-war down 'Queen of Scots' bearing down on Grantham with the blower eased back, smoke drifting from the chimney and steam at the safety valves. 'So what?' one might say. But the firebox would be full, and there would be enough in there, with the locomotive not extended, for Retford if not Doncaster, by which time the fire would have to be prepared for the West Riding gradients.

As a boy living at Leatherhead I saw little of the Brighton Atlantics on the Mid-Sussex route, and on my journey to or from Seaford on the school train they would appear but rarely; my sharpest memory is of passing Newhaven shed in a new Leyland bus in 1936 and seeing therein the cut-down, tough-looking Maunsell chimney of an Atlantic rather than the graceful Marsh pattern of which I was so fond. And it is on record that the Atlantics working on the Eastern Section from time to time, were well liked by most of the Chatham men who were used to nice big fires on some of their own locomotives, with sloping grates, and they did some very good work on the Ramsgate jobs before the War. And then, quite by chance on my way to Andover from Waterloo after a very early start from Doncaster back in 1943, we had an 'N15X' to Basingstoke, where, of all things, a Brighton Atlantic backed on with its Westinghouse pump at work — but where was that old pump? On Great Eastern locomotives the pump was on the gangway by the smokebox or ahead of the cab on the tender engines, an easy target for a blow with the hammer if the pump decided to refuse duty. But when I eventually traced the pump, one could see the top head and the lubricator between the frames and under the protruding smokebox. Whoever thought that one would never have to get down on his hands and knees at the age of 64 to fill the lubricator and as for the fitter

and his mate having to change the pump, words fail me but certainly not the men involved. But they were good running shed men who knew how to deal with impossible jobs as a matter of course and, come to think of it, it was probably lowered into a pit.

There were similarities in practice with the Great Northern locomotives: for example, the original saturated locomotives, Nos 37-41, had Richardson balanced slide valves and suffered from the same inability to get a train on the move. But whereas the GN men had to wrestle with a reversing lever, the Brighton locomotives had air reversers which helped the driver no end, provided they were in good order. My own experience of air reversers was on the GE Section on the D15 and D16 locomotives, which had both air and screw operation, a first-rate design, whereas the Marsh gear did present certain eccentricities to other than a loyal Brighton man. The slide-valve locomotives had the same reputation of getting away faster than the later piston-valve locomotives once on the move, and the King's Cross fireman of No 291, which remained a flat-valver to the end, told me that his locomotive was a minute faster to Finsbury Park than the similar piston-valve locomotive; this was back in 1923, long before he became a Loco Inspector.

The Brighton locomotives worked their share of the top-class work until the small-tender 'Arthurs' arrived in 1926., and in the longer term they made their name right up to the end at Newhaven on the boat trains, never mind the weekend

summer through workings to Willesden and Kensington — heavy old trains, most of them, and heavily loaded; they had easier timings than the Brighton-line expresses, but it was hard going 'up the Keymer', the junction with the main line at 15mph, almost immediately preceding the long climb to Balcombe.

In my time at Stewarts Lane, from 1952 to the end of 1954, the Newhaven Atlantics rarely came to the shed and the relief boat trains that we worked were largely with our own small-tender 'Arthurs' (N°s 30793-5) and our one 'Schools' (N° 30915). Nor did we see the Atlantics on West London work. The Newhaven men came up with a through train to the Midlands and points north with an Atlantic and stayed at either Willesden or Kensington for their return working, unless they went to Victoria to work a relief boat train. They had to lug their heavy trains up to North Pole and on to Willesden, and we used U1- or N-class Moguls working through to the coast from Willesden or Kensington. I cannot recall the remotest trouble with the Newhaven men and their locomotives; they came and went and never had to pay us a call! But the same cannot be said of those Newhaven men who had worked the 6.10pm Victoria–Uckfield, a 10-coach train in the evening rush hour with an Atlantic and night after night, the job was worked to time. So Waterloo gave the job to Stewarts Lane, which was diagrammed to work the 6.10 with an LMR Fairbairn tank engine, usually No 42106, which was out-

During Dick Hardy's period at Stewarts Lane depot, where he was the Shed Master there between August 1952 to January 1955, Britannia class Pacific locomotives Nº 70004 *William Shakespeare* and Nº 70014 *Iron Duke* were always cleaned to immaculate standards for use on the '*Golden Arrow*' and the 'second arrow' service, which left Victoria thirty minutes later at 14:30. Here we see Nº 70014 *Iron Duke* suitably adorned with its insignia, ready for another high-speed effortless run to Dover. (Antony M. Ford)

stationed at Newhaven in 1951. So the Newhaven men were aggrieved and the Stewarts Lane men in Nº 6 link, were far from happy especially with the injectors of their Fairbank tank and the need to waste time taking water at Oxted. So the 'Terrible 6.10' became a desperate struggle!

Enter the 'Earl of Ashurst', this being one of the nicknames of a certain Philip Evetts, a remarkably able student of railway affairs and a Newhaven Atlantic man through and through. Every evening, as the locomotive backed onto the 6.10 to Uckfield at Victoria, there would be the 'Earl' standing by the buffers, bowler hat, riding mackintosh, hands on hips, legs apart and a critical expression looking as if he had had a bad day at the Races. He had very strong views on the re-diagramming and maintained that Stewarts Lane men were not up to the job. He had written direct to Waterloo, so far without any action being taken, even when he gave the Motive Power Superintendent full details giving comparable timings by Atlantics and '4PTs', and telephoned me to meet him one evening at Victoria, and I had a pretty sharp dressing down for my pains. But, for all that, we began to develop a certain friendship. And so things settled down, and we gave as much attention to the running of the train as possible — until the fatal week!

Early in 1953 a certain driver of a nervous disposition and given to scenting trouble was on the 6.10, and for some reason the locomotive, instead of working empties up to Victoria, was booked straight up to Victoria light-engine. The

booked locomotive that worked up from Newhaven was an Atlantic, and our friend made very heavy work of the job, losing time from the start just getting up the 1 in 64 onto the bridge. Next evening the driver refused to take Nº 42106 due to faulty injectors and was given E1 Nº 1504, well stricken in miles but a splendid locomotive which would have done the job in the right hands. Ten bogies, no banker — Balham in nine, East Croydon in 18 minutes from Victoria. But this time the running was catastrophic. I cannot remember how I dealt with the driver, but I do know that he was rarely (if ever) in trouble again. As for me, my chief, Gordon Nicholson, instructed me to remove the turn from Nº 6 and place it where it should have been since 1951, in the top Brighton link, Nº 3, full of excellent men. The second part of the men's diagram included the up Horsham–Battersea goods with an 'N'-class Mogul, and Nº 3 (a passenger link) did not think much of that, but there we are — no more trouble.

Somehow I had to see what the Brighton Atlantics were really like, and one day up came Nº 32424 *Beachy Head* on 742 duty, and I made the time to go light-engine to Eardley for the coaches forming the 5.50pm Victoria–Tunbridge Wells and then drop onto the 6.10. The fireman, Denis Finch, had had a few firing trips, and the young Dual Link driver, Charlie Miles, likewise, which gave me time to compare the Brighton with the GN locomotive — and I was in for a shock. I knew, of course, that the LBSCR locomotives had always been left-hand drive, and, as I expected, the fire-hole was a GN trap door, to which I was well used. However, the reversing gear was a bulky air-operated affair rather than the crude lever on the GN locomotives, and the driver had the option of standing beside and across his bulky gear or sitting on top of it, a position preferred by quite a few. So far so good, but the actual operation of the gear was controlled by hand and air, and I understood that it was possible to learn the knack of operating what he could not actually see high up on his seat. But I am sure that the resourceful engine-men soon got top-side of the arrangement, for never a word of complaint did I hear.

And so at about 6pm Driver Tom Simmons and his mate arrived to take charge. Denis Finch had put a good back end on the fire exactly the same as on the GN locomotives, and the method of firing was to be exactly the same — but not so for me, because the locomotive was left-hand drive, and I had no room to work if I fired from the left; my background was on the GN, GE, GC, where all locomotives were right-hand drive. The air reversing gear took up most of the room on the driver's side, and Tom opted to sit above the gear right up — so it seemed — in the roof. This meant that I had to fire from the middle of the footplate and that my feeding of coal to the right-hand corners and sides of the firebox demanded a very powerful twist of the wrists. So, at 6.10 and after a lecture from the 'Earl of Ashurst' on the superiority of the Brighton locomotives, away we went up the 1 in 64 onto the bridge like a bat out of hell. Tom set the locomotive

at about 50 per cent with the regulator well open, and thanks to Denis Finch's back end and my firing somewhere the mark against the injector which held the boiler up very well, we were through 'Balham in nine' still on 200psi. But because of my awkward stance she was getting the better of me, and when Tom shut off before East Croydon I had only about 170psi. Unfortunately I had to get off at Croydon, but Tom's mate soon had the fire right, and they were on their way to Uckfield with the front six coaches. I have spoken to half a dozen of our firemen of the day, and they all agree that the Atlantics, in the right hands, were excellent locomotives. They agree that the driver operated 'upstairs' whilst they performed at a lower level held in by the huge cab doors; they also agree that a big fire at the back end, well burned through and made up with great care, was essential — as, indeed, it was on the GN Atlantics.

A grand locomotive, right up to the job and on which everything worked as it should, much better-riding than the GN locomotive, more powerful because the boiler could cope with the larger cylinders but not quite the world-beater into which the Robinson 32-element superheater had turner the Doncaster locomotive and in which, according to H. N. Gresley himself, superheated steam would reach well over 400?C, which is mighty hot.

So there we are — I had the great pleasure of travelling to Brighton and back in October 1952 behind Newhaven men in both directions. This was a fascinating day out and had a certain similarity to the

'Plant Centenarian' experience in 1953, when the two Atlantics were driven by ex-Great Central men. In 1952 N° 32424 was driven on the down road by Driver Turner, who originated from Dover, and on the way back by an ex-Slade Green driver, Ern Ecott. The old locomotive went like a good 'un throughout, with ex-SECR men who knew exactly what they were doing. You can see where my loyalties lie, for my great shed was originally Longhedge (LCDR) and then Battersea (SECR) before becoming Stewarts Lane (SR and, later, BR).

To conclude, let us see what Cecil J. Allen made of the Brighton Atlantics in 1929. He quotes from the letter from a Brighton engineering pupil gaining experience on the main line. He travelled on one of the earlier locomotives, No 40, which for some reason took the place of the usual and more powerful Baltic tank on the 8.45am Brighton–London Bridge, with Driver Tester of Brighton in charge. The train was made up of 10 corridor coaches and one First-class Pullman car, estimated at a total of 390 tons gross.

'N° 40 got away well, and they should have passed the Keymer in 13 minutes had not the locomotive slipped on a bad rail between Patcham and Clayton tunnels and again inside the latter. So they were half a minute late through Haywards Heath, but N° 40 was given the gun and passed Three Bridges half a minute ahead and Earlswood, one and a half ahead, but by then the locomotive had been drastically eased for the remainder of the climb to the Quarry. Despite

R. H. N. Hardy, Richard Hardy, or simply known by many as just Dick Hardy, had an illustrious career on the railways. He was an apprentice at Doncaster Works and forty years later was a divisional manager for British Railways. Dick has written extensively about his life and memories of the railway, as well as creating a unique and valuable collection of photographs of railwayman and locomotives from the 1930s onwards. (R. H. N. Hardy)

signal checks the train was only one and three quarter minutes late into London, and the net time was no more than 57 — a fine effort for an Atlantic with 390 tons. But what of the drastic easing? "With full regulator all the way to Balcombe No 40 was certainly worked hard, the cut-off being around 60 per cent to Keymer Junction and 50 per cent onwards with full regulator throughout and the noise of the beat at speed was tremendous." I should think so! Certainly hard going, but she stood on 200psi all the way thanks to the high-class work of the fireman. Were our friend's figures accurate? Was Driver Tester a lesser

Sparshatt? Was the so-called easing as drastic as made out? We shall never know, but I shall stick to my belief that, while the Brighton Atlantics were great locomotives, the old Ivatt C1s in their final, high-superheat form were world-beaters!'

By way of a 'PS' I include some notes written by Philip Evetts of the 6.10 service from Victoria to Uckfield, back in 1951, which were given to me many years ago:

'I have been unable to get to the bottom of the driver's seating arrangements of the Newhaven Atlantics, but I have discovered that an entirely unofficial modification enabled the driver to be seated at his work, although the problem was not completely solved. In the original design there was no seat on the driver's side, because there was no room to rig up the conventional hinged wooden seat, as all available room was occupied by the air-operated reversing gear, which also had a wheel for hand adjustment to the rear of the air gear and near the left-hand cab doors. So the Newhaven-based Atlantics had special removable seats made by the Marine Department at Newhaven Docks. It seems that whoever was in charge of Newhaven shed, had approached the Marine people, and between them they had concocted a sort of saddle resting on the sizeable

air brake casting and slotted down the middle lengthways so that the driver could see the figures on his reversing-gear rack and the position of the indicator. The driver then had the option of riding astride or sitting side-saddle! But for all that, the driver still had to get off his new seat to peer through the slot to alter the cut-off, which was a confounded nuisance or do it behind his back, which could be done, making sure that he did not loose his grip on the reversing wheel. Or he could find the right position — say 50 per cent — and do everything else on the regulator. So now the driver could ride his 'saddle' astride, until he needed to alter the cut-off or ride side-saddle with his legs dangling, slide off and do the whole operation from a standing position, before resuming his side-saddle posture.'

No wonder that the engine-men used to go miles at the same cut-off and all adjustments to power output were made by means of the regulator. This would be called 'altering the design of a locomotive without permission of the CME' and was, of course, regularly done. For if you wait for a CME, you wait for ever.

Dick Hardy
Amersham

BIBLIOGRAPHY

An Historical Survey of Southern Sheds by Chris Hawkins and George Reeve (Oxford Publishing Co, 1979)

Atlantic News — 'Reconstruction of 32424 *Beachy Head*' (various issues)

BR Steam Motive Power Depots: SR by Cecil J. Allen (Ian Allan, 1968)

The Bricklayers Arms Branch and Loco Shed by Michael Jackman (Oakwood Press, 1980)

British Atlantic Locomotives by Paul Bolger (Ian Allan, 1983)

British Railway Steam Locomotives 1948-1968 by Hugh Longworth (Oxford Publishing Co, 2005)

Great Locomotives of the Southern Railway by O. S. Nock (Guild Publishing, 1987)

The Gresley Observer (various issues)

History of Southern Locomotives to 1938 by C. S. Cocks (Institution of Locomotive Engineers, 1949)

LBSCR Stock Book by Peter Cooper (Runpast Publishing, 1990)

London, Brighton & South Coast Railway Miscellany by Kevin Robertson (Oxford Publishing Co, 2004)

The London, Brighton & South Coast Railway — The Bennett Collection by Klaus Marx (Lightmoor Press, 2011)

The Railway Magazine (various issues)

Roaming the Southern Rails by P. Ransome-Wallis (Ian Allan, 1979)

The West London Railway and the WLER by H. V. Borley and R. W. Kidner (Oakwood Press, 1975)

www.sixbellsjunction.co.uk

INDEX